BENNINGTON AND THE CIVIL WAR

Company A, Fourth Vermont Regiment. *Left to right*: Lucius Norton, Frederick Godfrey, Frederick Rogers and Nelson Otis Wilcox (age fourteen), sitting at camp before the battle at Lee's Mill, Virginia, April 1862.

Bennington and the Civil War

Bill Morgan

Published by The History Press
Charleston, SC 29403
www.historypress.net

Cover images courtesy of the Bennington Museum.

First published 2013

Manufactured in the United States

ISBN 978.1.62619.171.6

Library of Congress CIP data applied for.

Notice: The information in this book is true and complete to the best of our knowledge. It is offered without guarantee on the part of the author or The History Press. The author and The History Press disclaim all liability in connection with the use of this book.

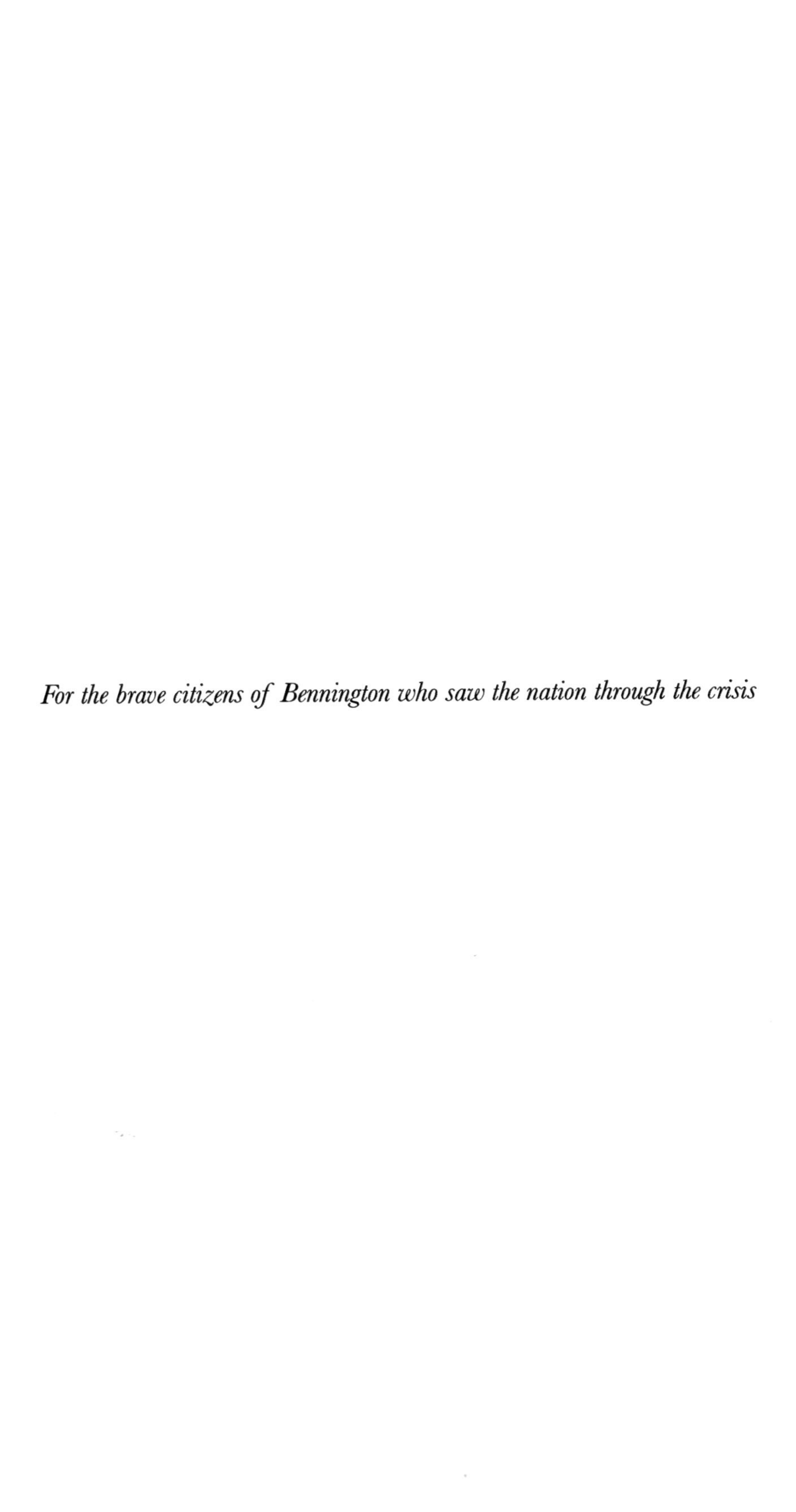

For the brave citizens of Bennington who saw the nation through the crisis

Contents

Acknowledgements

This book grew out of a bus tour designed by Anne Bugbee and myself for the Bennington Historical Society. In honor of the 150th anniversary of the Civil War, we decided to show our members around Bennington as it looked in 1861. The tour was so well received that Tyler Resch, the librarian of the Bennington Museum Library, suggested I write up the material as an article for the *Walloomsack Review*. Once he had the finished manuscript in hand, he was surprised by the amount of Civil War–related sites we had uncovered and suggested that The History Press might give the book a wider readership than his periodical, and so it came across the transom to the kind folks at that publisher. They suggested that the publication be timed to coincide with an exhibition at the Bennington Museum of Bennington in the Civil War years, and so it was that this volume came about.

Anne Bugbee has my everlasting thanks for her help on this and other projects of historical interest. She has read what seems like every book on Vermont history and is a font of information. She co-led the tours that gave birth to this paper. Without a doubt, Tyler Resch deserves all the credit for helping get this book into print. Without his suggestions, it never would have been anything but a Sunday afternoon tour.

Special thanks to the staff at The History Press, who worked hard to get this book out on time. Special thanks to Whitney Landis and Julia Turner who guided the manuscript through the maze of publishing specifications with untiring help.

Thanks also to the people at the Bennington Museum for their help in putting together the material and illustrations for the current volume. In particular, the museum's director, Robert Wolterstorff, and curator, Jamie Franklin, have been most helpful. Callie Stewart worked tirelessly to provide illustrations for the text, and I am in her debt. A good deal of the research was done with the help of the members of the Bennington Historical Society, Anne Bugbee, Joe Hall, Ted Bird and Charles Dewey. Robert Guarino, Bill Keogan, Mark Rondeau and Venus Van Ness have all been generous with their time and their knowledge.

Finally, never-ending praise must go to my secret editor, my wife, Judy Matz. Without her careful attention to the words, this manuscript would scarcely be more than incoherent ramblings.

Introduction

Although we in Bennington think of the Revolutionary War as "our war" and the famous Battle of Bennington along the banks of the Walloomsac River as "our battle," it was not the war in which the greatest number of Bennington men fought and died. And although the graveyard beside the Old First Church is filled with flags honoring our Revolutionary War heroes, those are but a fraction of the number of graves of the brave Civil War veterans that populate the town's many cemeteries.

The years 2011 to 2015 mark the sesquicentennial anniversary of the American Civil War. As such, considerable attention has been focused on the states in which the great battles of that war took place. However, in tens of thousands of towns across the country, both North and South, another battle was being fought during the Civil War years, and Bennington was no exception. This was the battle on the homefront, and Bennington's participants were the parents, wives, children and loved ones of the soldiers who were risking their lives to preserve the Union in combat. They were the people who watched their "boys" go off to war, perhaps never to return or to return with scars and wounds that would never heal. For four long years people read the pages of the *Bennington Banner* (a weekly newspaper in those days), hoping that the names of their loved ones would not appear in the columns listing the casualties. The story of Bennington during the Civil War years is a part of our national history just as much as that of Gettysburg and Fredericksburg. It seems fitting now to remember those people and places that played such an important role in that history.

Part I

Bennington and the Civil War

Slavery

A little background to the war would seem appropriate to help set the stage. In an effort to be brief, it must be an oversimplification of complex issues. I refer readers to the works of Benedict, Waite and Crockett, as well as the more recent books by Howard Coffin listed in the bibliography for more complete accounts. Those books document the deeds of Vermonters during the "Great Rebellion," as the Civil War was called at the time. However, any discussion of the role Bennington played in the conflict is meaningless without first examining the larger story of state and national events.

Although the Civil War raged across the country from 1861 until 1865, it had roots that extended back much further. The issue of slavery had divided the country since its very beginning. As developing territories became new states, a series of compromises helped to maintain the balance of power between slave and free states. Equal representation was unsustainable in the long run, as growing populations in the North were fed by immigration and industrialization. It became clear that eventually the South would be in the minority in every way.

The debate over slavery had been raging for many decades, long before Abraham Lincoln was elected president or South Carolina seceded, taking ten other states with it. Most Vermonters, and most Benningtonians, were determined to keep the Union together and had reluctantly accepted compromises with slave states for the sake of peace and unity. Any attempts to break the Union were considered treasonous throughout much of New England.

The freeing of Dinah Mattis. *Author's collection.*

From the outset, the abolitionist spirit was very strong throughout Vermont. Interestingly enough, in a census taken of the state in 1772, there were a total of sixteen slaves listed, and all of them lived in Bennington.[1] Vermont was the first state to outlaw slavery in its Constitution, which was written in 1777. The first article of that document begins: "That all men are born equally free and independent…therefore no male person born in this country, or brought from over seas, ought to be holden by law, to serve any person as a servant, slave, or apprentice, after he arrives at the age of twenty-one years."[2]

In November 1779, during the later stages of the Revolutionary War, Captain Ebenezer Allen led a raid against the British along the Boquet River in New York near Lake Champlain. He returned to Vermont with a slave, Dinah Mattis, and her two-month-old daughter, Nancy, captured from the enemy. In addition to liberating them from their masters, Captain Allen gave Mattis a document proclaiming their freedom. She brought that paper to Bennington's town clerk, Moses Robinson, and was issued a proper certificate of freedom.[3] The reading of Mattis's emancipation letter is depicted in a highly romanticized mural in the Rutland Post Office, which was painted in 1937 by Stephen Belaski. For comparison's sake, remember that in 1778, the Massachusetts State Constitution clearly recognized slavery as a legal institution, and New York State did not abolish slavery until 1827, a full fifty years after Vermont. It is interesting also to note that Reverend David Avery, the second minister at the First Congregational Church, had created a controversy in Bennington by bringing his own slave with him while he served as minister from 1780 until 1783. One of his parishioners was excommunicated from the church for refusing to acknowledge the pastor's right to hold a slave, but eventually, the congregation forced Avery's resignation in May 1783.[4]

William Lloyd Garrison. *Author's collection.*

Howard Coffin, Vermont's great contemporary Civil War scholar, suggests that the Civil War might not have begun for Vermont when the first shots were fired on Fort Sumter. Nor did it begin in Windsor on that stormy July 1777 morning when the Vermont constitution was drawn up but rather in Old Bennington in 1828. It was in that year that William Lloyd Garrison arrived to found the *Journal of the Times*, a newspaper dedicated to three causes. "We have three objects in view, which we shall pursue through life, whether in this place or elsewhere," Garrison wrote in the first issue. "Namely, the suppression of intemperance and its associated vices, the gradual emancipation of every slave in the Republic, and the perpetuity of national peace."[5] He remained in town for less than a year, but it was Garrison who went on to create the most influential abolitionist newspaper in the country, the *Liberator*. It was through the pages of the *Liberator* that the flames of abolition were fanned, eventually blazing into war.

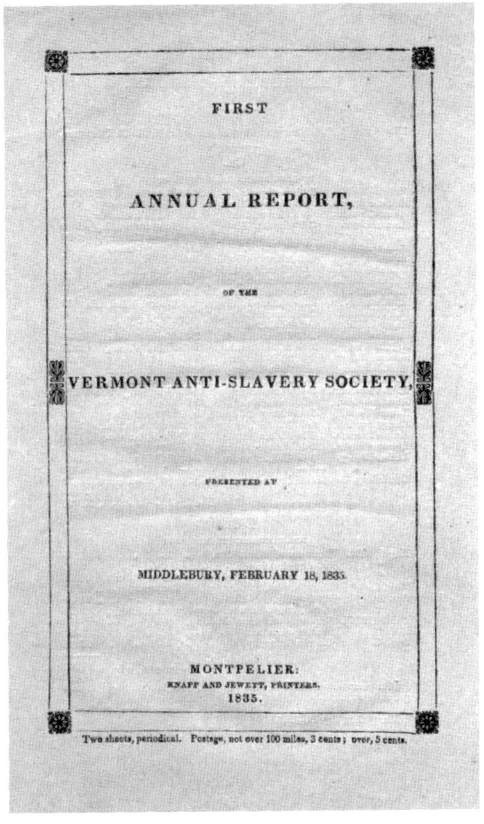

FIRST

ANNUAL REPORT,

OF THE

VERMONT ANTI-SLAVERY SOCIETY,

PRESENTED AT

MIDDLEBURY, FEBRUARY 18, 1835.

MONTPELIER:
KNAPP AND JEWETT, PRINTERS.
1835.

Two sheets, periodical. Postage, not over 100 miles, 3 cents; over, 5 cents.

First annual report of the Vermont Anti-Slavery Society, 1835. *Bennington Museum, Bennington, Vermont.*

In 1833, the state's first antislavery society was organized on the other side of the mountain in Jamaica, Vermont. Within a year, there were twenty such organizations active in the state. John Myers, the eminent historian, wrote, "A good case can be made for the thesis that Vermont became the first state to readily accept abolitionist doctrines."[6] Even after Garrison left for Baltimore, he would return to Vermont on speaking tours as did other staunch abolitionists, such as Frederick Douglass and Wendell Phillips. By 1846, the *Rutland Herald* estimated that 80 percent of Vermonters were opposed to slavery.[7]

In the years before the war, the Underground Railroad was busy in Vermont. This was a more or less informal group of antislavery activists who assisted runaway slaves on their way north to find freedom in Canada.[8] One popular route appears to have entered Bennington County along the road from Troy and, thus, passed through this area before turning north to Rutland, Brandon and Burlington. Little actual documentation exists, since this was a highly secret operation and it would have been unwise for anyone

Home of Charles Hicks. *Author's collection.*

to keep written records. Evidence does indicate that one local safe house was operated by the stagecoach driver Charles Hicks, who had a ninety-one-acre farm near the intersection of today's Rice Lane and Matteson Road. A rare documented case indicates that in 1843, a black slave traveling with his wife and three children stopped overnight in Hicks's farmhouse, and in the morning, Hicks's son guided them to another safe house in Shaftsbury.[9] Although there are local legends about secret caves on Mount Anthony and hidden rooms in old houses, this seems to be the only credible site we know of today.[10]

Vermont Prepares for War

By December 5, 1859, when John Brown's body passed through the North Bennington train depot en route to burial on his farm in North Elba, New York, virtually all hope for any peaceful solution had been extinguished.[11] Only a handful of Vermonters still felt that it was possible to avert a crisis. One of them was Hiland Hall, who served two one-year terms as governor from October 1858 through October 1860. Hall, who lived on Park Street in North Bennington, was an outspoken critic of slavery, and in his first speech as governor, he denounced the Dred Scott decision. That ruling basically said that any slave who lived in a free state was still a slave and must be considered as such. That meant that Vermont officials were bound by law to recognize the institution of slavery and participate in the apprehension of runaways. Hall said that this was "contrary to the plain language of the Vermont Constitution, to the facts of history, and to the dictates of common humanity."[12]

When the State of Virginia called for a "Peace Congress" in February 1861, on the eve of the Civil War, some saw it as a last-ditch effort to avert war. Others believed it was only a diversionary tactic for the purpose of buying time so that the South could arm itself and prepare its troops for battle. When Vermont's elected congressional representatives refused to attend the congress, Governor Erastus Fairbanks asked ex-Governor Hall to head the state's delegation. Although they met in Washington from February 4 to 21, nothing came of it.[13] Many local people believed that Hall had been

Hiland Hall. *Bennington Museum, Bennington, Vermont.*

Governor Erastus Fairbanks. *Bennington Museum, Bennington, Vermont.*

used as a pawn in the South's plot against the Union, and his reputation suffered as a result. However, when the conflict erupted into war, no one supported the Union more than Hiland Hall.

The census of 1860 lists Vermont's population at 315,827 (today, it is just about double that, at 626,000). The town of Bennington's population was 4,389 while the whole county numbered 19,436.[14] During the war, nearly 34,238 men enlisted statewide, probably between one-third and one-half of the male population that was eligible to serve in the army, an incredibly high percentage. Of these, 5,124 died as a result of wounds or disease. There are no accurate records of the number wounded, but it would have been in the range of another 10,000 men. We do know that 5,022 men were discharged due to their wounds. During the war, Vermont's ratio of men killed per capita was second only to Michigan's, and some accounts even give Vermont the unfortunate distinction of being the highest. Either way, it was a very costly war for both Vermont and

Bennington. By the end of four years, the town of Bennington had sent over 400 troops to combat, and Bennington County had sent nearly 1,000 men to war.[15]

General Winfield Scott. *Author's collection.*

In the spring of 1861, the North found itself completely unprepared for war. The nation's standing army counted only sixteen thousand men, and they were scattered mainly throughout the western territories, where they had seen only limited action in skirmishes with Native American tribes.[16] The commanding general at the time was seventy-four-year-old Winfield Scott, who had been a soldier since 1808. Although he was still mentally able to command, he had numerous illnesses, and it was rumored that he was too feeble to even mount his horse. The Union army was also ill prepared to fight. Politically, it would have appeared provocative to build up the military in anticipation of a fight with the Southern states, since they were still part of the United States. So General Scott's hands were tied until the actual opening volley was fired. In fairness to the general's intelligence, it should also be noted that his original strategy, which he proposed at the outbreak of the war and called the Anaconda Plan, was the strategy that eventually brought victory four years later. It called for a protracted blockade and eventual strangulation and dissection of the South. Initially, no one believed the rebellion would last more than a few months, so his proposal wasn't given much credence in Washington.

War Is Declared

Everything changed for the country and for Bennington on April 12, 1861, when South Carolina artillery opened fire on Fort Sumter, the fort designed to protect Charleston Harbor. The Civil War had begun. It took a day or two for the news to reach Bennington, but when it did, the citizens responded immediately.

On April 15, President Lincoln called for seventy-five thousand volunteers to enlist in the army for three months. His initial fear was that Washington, right in the middle of enemy territory, might quickly fall into the hands of the Rebels. Governor Fairbanks called for the general assembly to convene in a special session on April 23, but even before that session convened, towns across the state were already holding public meetings. On April 19, 1861, a meeting was held at Bennington's Apollo Hall, one of the largest meeting halls in town, located near the Four Corners on today's Route 7. The following night, another meeting was held in the same auditorium for the purpose of forming a militia.[17]

Before the first meeting, a large American flag was hung over the town's main thoroughfare. Bennington's Cornet Band played patriotic songs, and everyone in attendance unanimously pledged to support the Union. Then ex-Governor Hiland Hall called the meeting to order. It was announced that "four sons of Bennington" had left that day to join the army. After several patriotic speeches, the meeting adjourned with three cheers for the Union and the Constitution, followed by a singing of "The Star-Spangled Banner,"

The attack on Fort Sumter. *Author's collection.*

which was not yet our national anthem (and wouldn't be until 1931).[18] The initial problem was that there was no organized army for men to join. Traditionally, each town in Vermont had supported its own militia consisting of local men who drilled together on a regular basis. Over the decades of peace, these militias, where they still existed, had become little more than social groups. Bennington's militia had long since disbanded. When Hiland Hall was serving as governor in 1860, he had called for a muster of the state's militia, and only nine hundred men appeared in Montpelier. The state inventory records show that there were 957 antique muskets, 6 field pieces and 503 all but useless Colt pistols in the arsenal. The local militia units that still existed were disorganized and were not in effective fighting condition, according to all reports. With President Lincoln's call for troops, men were suddenly training everywhere. By the fall of 1861, five thousand Vermont men had responded and were enlisted in the army.[19]

On April 23, 1861, the Vermont General Assembly, which had been asked by the U.S. secretary of war, Simon Cameron, to raise one regiment of 780 men, voted instead to raise seven regiments. When a motion was made to authorize an expenditure of $500,000 for these troops, they voted to use $1 million instead. The state also decided to pay each private $7 per month in addition to the $13-per-month salary paid by the federal government.[20] With the initial call to arms, all existing militia were ordered to rendezvous in Rutland on May 2, and they were mustered in a week later as the First Vermont Regiment. On that same day, May 7, 1861, they left Vermont for Virginia. A few men from Bennington who had previous military training were with them, but the bulk of Bennington volunteers had to wait until the Second Regiment was formed the following month. Since everyone expected the war to be brief, the First Vermont was mustered in for only ninety days. On August 15, 1861, those men returned home via Brattleboro, where they were mustered out of the army. To their credit, most of the men of the First Regiment immediately reenlisted for an additional three years' tour of duty with other units.

Bennington Volunteers for Duty

Back in Bennington, the first volunteer company, whose goal was to put one hundred men in the field, quickly formed. Officially, the company called itself the Bennington Union Guards, but it soon adopted the nickname of "the Bennington Boys." As the first company to sign up and fill its quota, it became Company A of the Second Vermont Regiment, a distinction in which the whole town took considerable pride. Each volunteer needed to be at least twenty-one years old or have the consent of his parents, and he needed to be at least five feet, four inches tall. They drilled seven hours a day under Sergeant Finney, a member of Brandon, Vermont's "Allen Guards." In the first days of the war, it was difficult to find experienced soldiers locally for the purpose of training troops. The men of Company A voted for their officers and chose Captain James H. Walbridge of Bennington to lead them. Newton Stone was made first lieutenant, G.S. Ladd second lieutenant and William H. Cady third lieutenant.

The large hall at the Gates Hotel was turned into a "vast tailoring establishment," charged with making uniforms for the town's volunteers as quickly as possible. A.M. Day generously offered his time and services to head the team of tailors and seamstresses.[21] Because there were no regulation uniforms at the beginning of the war, many of them were made of gray cloth until the state issued orders that they must all be blue.

It seemed that everyone in town was eager to volunteer or contribute in some way. The ladies of Bennington immediately set about making a

large ceremonial flag that was to be presented to the troops. They met in another of the town's hotels, the Franklin House, and in the early weeks of the war, they created the flag that is still in the collection of the Bennington Museum today. On the stripes they embroidered the words, "Presented to the Bennington Boys of '61 by the Ladies."[22] That flag was used frequently in town parades but was never carried into battle. It was also used in ceremonies for decades after the war and was commonly seen draped over the coffins at each veteran's funeral. The last surviving Civil War veterans, John C. Clark and E. Payson Hathaway, gave it to the Bennington Museum in 1929. In May 1861, the flag was presented to Company A at the Old First Church after the 77 members of the Bennington Union Guard were officially mustered in by General Hopkins. Even then, Captain Walbridge continued to recruit, since a company needed to number between 83 and 101 men.[23]

Like other towns, the people of Bennington pulled together in support of its troops. Meetings were held regularly in Armory Hall, part of the Wheeler Building, which once stood on the site of today's public library. Through these meetings, the citizenry was kept informed about the progress of war and the preparations being made in Bennington. Everyone did what he could to show his patriotism. The students of the Mount Anthony Seminary raised the Stars and Stripes in a sign of solidarity with the Union, and the town ordered the purchase of a large 12- by 20-foot flag to be flown from a new 124-foot-tall flagpole being erected in front of the Gates Hotel. That hotel was located near the East Main Street entrance to the Village Cemetery. When the flag arrived, it was raised above the village after an afternoon of patriotic speeches. A U.S. coat of arms was placed above the courthouse, which, in 1861, stood next to the First Congregational Church, roughly where the McCullough mausoleum stands today.[24]

The entire Second Vermont Regiment, including Bennington's Company A, rendezvoused in Burlington on June 20, 1861, and left the state on June 24. They saw action on July 21 at the first battle of Bull Run, and when the defeat of the Union army turned into a rout, Company

Opposite, top: Officers of Company A, Second Vermont Regiment, circa 1861. *Standing, left to right*: Eugene O. Cole, Charles M. Bliss, William H. Cady, William Robinson, Edward W. Appleton and Newton Stone. *Seated, left to right*: two unidentified men, Abel K. Parsons, James H. Walbridge and Guilford S. Ladd. *Bennington Museum, Bennington, Vermont.*

Opposite, bottom: Gates' Hotel, East Main Street. *Bennington Museum, Bennington, Vermont.*

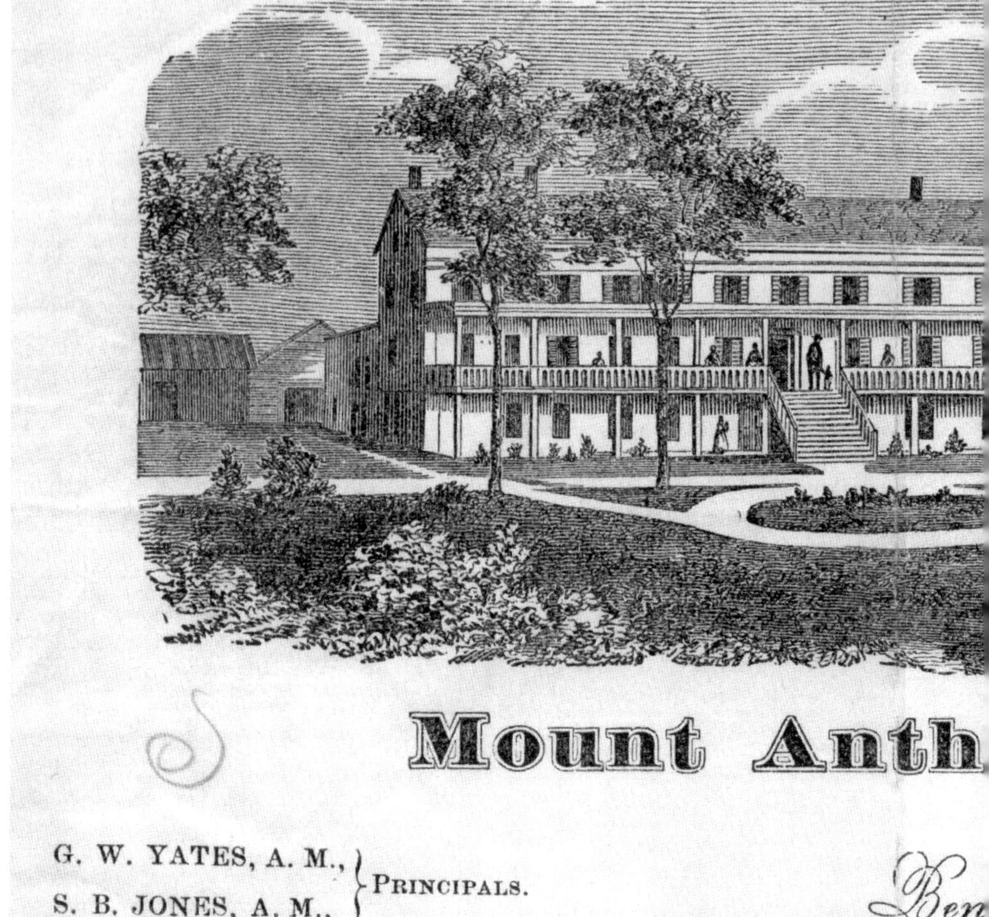

Mount Anthony Seminary. *Bennington Museum, Bennington, Vermont.*

A bravely refused to leave the battlefield. Bull Run proved to everyone that the war would be a long, bloody conflict. The Second Vermont was destined to fight with the Army of the Potomac in most of the battles in the eastern theater of the war.[25]

However, Company A was not the only company of soldiers being recruited in Bennington at the time. About fifty men met at Apollo Hall in late May for the purpose of forming a company of Zouaves. The Zouaves

were infantry units patterned after French troops known for their colorful Turkish-style uniforms and precision drilling. Bennington's Zouaves chose John E. Pratt as their captain and Charles Benton as lieutenant. Some of the town's most prominent men supported them financially and paid for their uniforms; among the financiers were Elyah Dewey, John Kehoe, Olin Scott, and Thomas J. Tiffany.[26]

Patriotism was also used as a pretext for celebrating and rowdy behavior. One group of men got together at Dennis Burke's home on Pottery Street (today's Park Street) for the purpose of raising their own flagpole. On May

Zouaves in uniform. *Author's collection.*

30, 1861, the *Bennington Banner* reported that the men decided that they would fire a cannon as part of their celebration. It isn't clear where they found a cannon, but they certainly didn't have the experience needed to use it. Either due to ignorance or to the alcoholic refreshments they were enjoying, they forgot to move a powder keg that was sitting in front of the cannon, and when the cannon was fired, the keg of gunpowder exploded, too. One celebrant was burned on the face, and another had all the hair scorched off his head.

Local industries and individual businessmen alike backed the Union cause. Some, such as the Bennington Powder Company, worked overtime to fill government orders.[27] Even before the war, the factories in town had begun to expand until they reached their peak of employment in the years

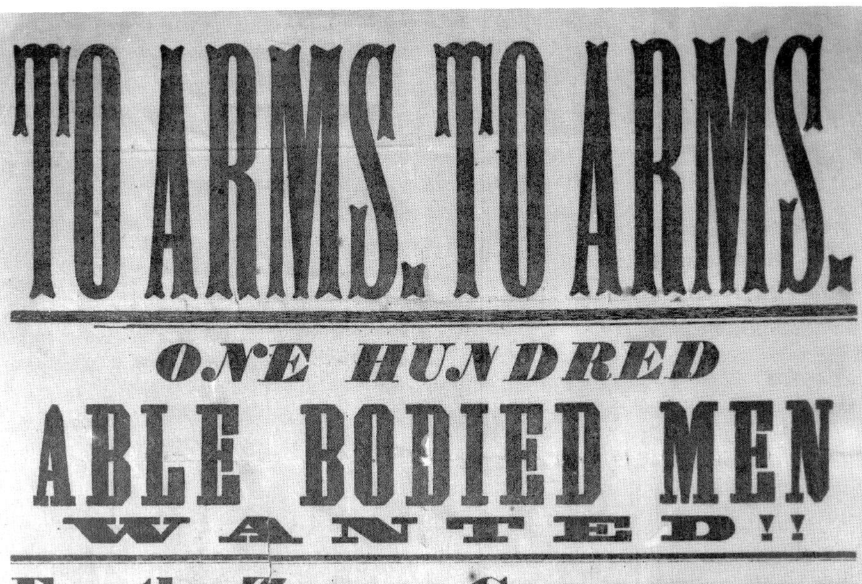
TO ARMS. TO ARMS.

ONE HUNDRED

ABLE BODIED MEN

WANTED!!

For the Zouave Company now being organized in Bennington, and soon to join the

First Zouave Regiment

of Vermont, to be mustered into the State service as soon as the same shall be filled--to serve three years unless sooner discharged.

Those who enlist in this Company will receive the full pay of United States' soldiers, and seven dollars per month additional from the State. They will also be entitled to the bounty lands and additional pay, granted by the United States to volunteers.

This Regiment will be supplied with the latest improved arms.

J. E. PRATT.

Recruiting Officer.

Bennington, August 10th, 1861.

Recruiting poster for Pratt's Zouave Regiment. *Bennington Museum, Bennington, Vermont.*

right after the war. The town's population surged nearly 35 percent during the 1860s to become 5,760 in 1870. This growth occurred in spite of the fact that many workers were lost due to recruitments. A directory from the end of the decade lists twenty manufacturers in town, nearly forty stores, several

Left: Colonel John Pratt. *Bennington Museum, Bennington, Vermont.*

Below: The Death of Colonel Elmer Ellsworth. *Frank Leslie's magazine, collection of the author.*

hotels, three livery stables, two druggists, five lawyers and three doctors. The cotton and woolen mills produced knit goods such as blankets, shirts, pants, shawls and underwear. Other mills and foundries employed a number of workers as well. By 1870, 400 people were employed by the woolen mills, 100 made carpenter squares, 65 were engaged in papermaking and 60 more in the foundries. An additional 20 to 30 worked in Bennington's famous pottery yards.[28]

On May 24, 1861, two months before Bull Run, Colonel Elmer Ellsworth of New York became the first officer to be killed by a Rebel when he was shot trying to remove a Confederate flag that was flying over a hotel in Alexandria, Virginia. The death of Ellsworth became a national tragedy, and all flags in Bennington were lowered to half-mast in his honor. It made it clear to people that the war would not end without loss of life, yet no one could imagine the carnage of what was to come. Reports from soldiers on the front lines began to appear in the pages of the *Bennington Banner*. Some men with ties to Bennington were already serving with troops from other states, and the names of many local men were listed with Massachusetts and New York regiments.[29]

Bennington Divided

Surprisingly, not all local men chose to fight for the Union. Although the overwhelming majority of Bennington residents wholeheartedly supported the North, some did not. The April 18, 1861 *Banner* pointed out that there were a number of secessionists in town, including people whose "ancestral lineage took active part in the Revolution." The editor was more than a bit shocked to hear that some local men even called for a Jeff Davis brigade to be formed of Northern men willing to fight for the Southern cause. The newspaper did not name names, but one prominent family that did see two of its sons join the Confederate army was the Robinsons. Uel Robinson raised his two boys, Charles and Frederick, in a house that still stands on Monument Avenue. When the war began, Charles was living in North Carolina and married to a local girl there. His eighteen-year-old younger brother, Fred, went south and joined him, and together they enlisted to fight for the Confederacy. It couldn't have made their relatives back in Bennington very happy when Fred wrote home and said that if he "had a thousand lives he would yield them all up to the confederacy."[30] The Robinson brothers took part in many battles and were both taken prisoner near the end of the war at the Battle of Bentonville. After the war, they both decided to remain in North Carolina and eventually were buried there. On June 13, 1861, the *Banner* also reported that George F. Thatcher of Bennington had enlisted with the Confederates after having spent his last few years teaching in the South.

Another interesting story of a Benningtonian who went south concerns Armand Edward Blackmar (1826–1888), born into one of Bennington's

Home of Uel Robinson. *Author's collection.*

most prominent families. Armand is actually famous for two reasons. First, he created an opening move in the game of chess that has become well known and is called "Blackmar's Gambit." In addition to being a chess master, Blackmar became the leading publisher of music in the South during the Civil War era. In 1837, while still a young boy, his family moved to Cleveland. There, Armand attended Western Reserve College before moving to Louisiana to teach music. When war broke out, he stayed in New Orleans and began to publish all the Confederate tunes that were popular in the South. Songs like the "Dixie War Song," "Southern Marseillaise" and "Beauregard Manassas" are examples of his work. He even wrote a popular song that many of us know called "Goober Peas." When the Union general Ben Butler occupied New Orleans, he arrested Blackmar for publishing "seditious" music and put him out of business, but after the war, Blackmar prospered again. To prove that he wasn't a Northerner caught accidentally in the South, when his daughter was born in 1861, Blackmar gave her the name "Louisiana Rebel Blackmar." These cases were exceptions, however, because the majority of people in Bennington were not sympathetic to the Rebel cause.[31]

Recruiting and Filling the Ranks

Throughout the war, recruiters were busy in Bennington creating new fighting units and replacing men in older units. New soldiers were continually needed to keep the regiments at full strength. The ranks were thinned not just by combat injuries but also by desertion and disease. In fact, more soldiers died as a result of disease during the Civil War than wounds caused from enemy fire. Things like dysentery, typhoid, pneumonia, tuberculosis, malaria and even measles were major causes of death.

Regimental histories can make for dry reading, but it is important to outline the basic structure of the Union army in order to appreciate all the companies, regiments and brigades commemorated on local memorials. The military was complex by the very nature of its organization. Not all Bennington men fought in Bennington units, and even Bennington units were not staffed entirely by men from town. There were Bennington men who fought with units from other counties and even other states. There were local men who were in the regular army and navy, too, and not part of the state's volunteer regiments. There were veterans of the Civil War who only came to Bennington after the war, and they also made significant contributions to the town's history. At least two men who were awarded the Medal of Honor (the precursor of the Congressional Medal of Honor) lived in town for significant periods after the war, but they were born and raised elsewhere.

As mentioned earlier, the First Vermont Regiment was formed from the state's standing militia and served for three months at the very beginning of

Company A, Fourth Vermont Regiment, stopping in Wilmington on its way to Brattleboro in September 1861. *Bennington Museum, Bennington, Vermont.*

the war. Since Bennington had no militia, few Benningtonians were in that unit, but those who were saw action at the Battle of Big Bethel in June 1861, which ended in a Union defeat. Of the 782 men in that unit, over 600 of them reenlisted at the end of their three-month tour.

The Second Vermont Regiment was the first nonmilitia volunteer force to respond to President Lincoln's call to arms, and Bennington was proud to organize the first company of that regiment, Company A. It was placed under the command of Captain James H. Walbridge of Bennington. Of the regiment's nearly 1,900 officers and men, over 750 were killed, wounded or died of disease. As those soldiers marched off to war, each man wore a sprig of evergreen in his cap, emblematic of his home state.[32]

Then, in the late summer, the Fourth Vermont Regiment was recruited from southern Vermont. The regiment was mustered in during September 1861 and was immediately dispatched to Washington. Bennington's John Halsey Cushman was appointed the quartermaster. In July 1861, Captain John E. Pratt began recruiting Bennington men for a company of Zouaves, and they were mustered in as Company A of the Fourth Vermont Regiment. On September 14, these men left Bennington heading for a camp in Brattleboro on wagons loaned by local teamsters, Norton and Sheldon. There the men were issued

Left: Major William D. Collins of the First Vermont Cavalry. *Bennington Museum, Bennington, Vermont.*

Below: Second Vermont Regimental Band, June 15, 1861. *Bennington Museum, Bennington, Vermont.*

Enfield rifles before being sent south via train. In fact, the newspaper reported that there were too many men eager to go along and four of them had to be sent back to Bennington the following day.

That September and October, Major Moses Harrington was busy in Bennington recruiting a company of cavalry soldiers. When his health failed, he was replaced by John V. Hall. They formed Company G of the First Vermont Cavalry Regiment, composed mainly of Bennington men. They were led by Captain James A. Sheldon, Lieutenant George H. Bean and Second Lieutenant Dennis M. Blackmer. In November, William D. Collins of Bennington was appointed major of the First Vermont Cavalry. This became the third company of men sent from Bennington, in addition to a group of twenty-five men who had joined Colonel Ramsey's New York Regiment. There was also a thirty-man regimental band formed in Bennington by F.M. Crossett.

During the following year, in the autumn of 1862, Company E of the Tenth Vermont Regiment was organized in Bennington to serve for three years. The men elected Madison E. Winslow as their captain. Although patriotism was still running high, the number of able volunteers was shrinking. As the Tenth Regiment was being formed, the town decided to offer a bounty of fifty dollars for each new recruit. "You are needed to thrash out Rebellion and restore things as they were and ought to be now," read the *Banner's* editorial in support of the call for additional troops.

The next to last Bennington volunteer unit to be mustered in was on October 21, 1862, when Company A of the Fourteenth Vermont Regiment was formed. The company was led by Captain Ransom O. Gore of Bennington. The men had been recruited for a term of only nine months, so by the end of July 1863, just after the Battle of Gettysburg, they were free to return home.

Then in April 1864, the final group of Bennington recruits formed Company F of the Seventeenth Vermont Regiment. They were led by Captain Lyman E. Knapp of Townshend, but his first lieutenant was George Hicks and his third sergeant was Samuel B. Norton, both Bennington men.

By consulting the numerous regimental histories of each of these units, it is easy to trace the battles in which men from Bennington fought. Suffice it to say that all these units saw a great deal of action throughout the war, mostly in the Virginia campaigns.

The Draft and Bounties

When the number of volunteers threatened to dry up in 1863, President Lincoln was forced to impose a draft to fill the ranks. Many towns offered bonuses and incentives so that men would enlist voluntarily; that way, municipalities would not have to enforce the draft. Although Bennington came close to filling its quota in the summer of 1863, about twenty-nine men were still needed. Men who were drafted were then given the option of serving in the army or paying a $300 fee as a bounty for a replacement. Some of Bennington's draftees who could afford to do so exercised that option and paid for substitutes. This was the same draft that would spark the bloody draft riots of July 1863 in New York City. Poor people were obviously unable to buy their way out of military service and were therefore disproportionately subject to conscription, and in some cities, violence erupted as a result. In

Abraham Lincoln. *Author's collection.*

HONOR TO THE BRAVE!!

The Governor of the State of Vermont has issued orders for the formation of two more Regiments of Volunteers, to serve in the army of the United States, for three years, unless sooner discharged by the termination of the war.

The response to this last call, and the seeming indifference to its importance, and the apparent lack of a hearty, prompt and enthusiastic response to the Executive requisition, are the points I would suggest for consideration.

In an hour of conflict, when our brothers, neighbors and friends, are heroically treading the historical plains of Yorktown, and breasting with unbroken front and undaunted courage the merciless foe, at the very foot of his strongholds, and driving them at the point of the bayonet, on and across ravines, swamps, woods and beyond the Chickahominy, and are now within the very sight of that Rebel Hades of our country, is it a time to sit in listless unconcern for the safety of those noble sons of these New England hills and valleys? Are we to be reckoned with those who, seeing danger to them, shun the responsibility of their rescue?

Are we, as the descendents of the immortal sires of '76, when the clarion war cry was, as now,

TO ARMS! TO ARMS!

to lie supinely upon our backs, in cool indifference to the danger of our kindred and friends before rebel columns of Southern conspirators? Or, like our sires, shall we not leave store and workshop, the plough and anvil, and meet, like veterans, the enemy of our nationality, these inhuman fiends, whose tinkling ornaments are the anatomical sections of our martyred dead, whose festal drinking cups are the sculls of our sons and brothers?

GREAT GOD! shall the sons of Vermont be found wanting, as the instruments in Thy hands, to avenge such inhumanities? Rather than falter now, at the call of our Executive; at the call of the President; at the call of an outraged civilization; we had better lie down, and die ignominiously —as die we should in the same way—if conquered without resistance, by this blood-stained slave Oligarchy of the South.

TO ARMS! THEN, YE SONS OF VERMONT!

FILL THE RANKS, AND LET US "ONWARD TO RICHMOND!" THE HOUR IS AT HAND!

Amid the thunders of McCLELLAN's ordnance, and the tramp of his victorious legions before Richmond, let us be found. A nobler work never fell to the lot of man than the work of sustaining the supremacy of a Free Government.

TO THE ARMY OF THE POTOMAC, THEN, LET US HASTEN! STRIKE FOR VICTORY! STRIKE FOR AND WITH McCLELLAN, AND THE VICTORY IS OURS!

A. SOLDIER.

Bennington, Vt., June 24, 1862.

Recruitment poster, June 24, 1862. *Bennington Museum, Bennington, Vermont.*

Bennington, no such trouble was reported because several procedures had been put in place to avoid any problems. First, the town provided the large bounty to help secure volunteer recruits. With enough volunteers, they would not have to resort to an unpopular draft lottery. Also, many men of modest means bought draft insurance, whereby for a smaller amount, they pooled their resources. Then if they were drafted, the $300 bounty fee was paid by the collective for their substitutes.

Inevitably, the process of paying large bounties created new problems. In Bennington, some men were happy to receive the incentive money and voluntarily fulfilled their military commitment. However, some less scrupulous men accepted the money and then deserted. Often they turned up later in another town to accept another bounty and so on, until they were apprehended. Desertion also became a bigger problem as the war dragged on. Usually, when caught, the deserters were returned to their units or imprisoned. Occasionally, they were hanged in order to send a clear message to others that desertion would not be tolerated. Anyone who has read *The Red Badge of Courage* will know just how easy it was to walk away from the army in those days.

1861

At the beginning of the war, these problems were still far in the future. Men were ready, willing and able to volunteer, and everyone felt that the war would be over within a matter of a few months. On Thursday, June 6, 1861, the Bennington Union Guards (Company A of the Second Vermont Regiment) marched down Main Street from the Armory in the Wheeler building to the railroad depot. Hundreds gathered along the street waving flags and cheering. Captain F.M. Crossett led the Bennington Cornet Band as they marched along with Company A.[33] They played patriotic songs while the troops boarded the train to Burlington, where they would rendezvous with the other companies of the Second Vermont. The thirty members of the band were scheduled to depart for the front a few days later amid similar fanfare. Before they left town, they gave one last concert at Wheeler Hall, where they were awarded three cheers from the crowd. The *Banner* reported that the "Boys Have Gone," but they would not be the last to go by any means.[34]

Letters also began to arrive from members of the First Vermont that spoke of how things on the front lines were less than perfect. By then the First had arrived at Fort Monroe, Virginia, and reports said that although money was available, the men still suffered from lack of blankets and good food.[35] Logistically, it would take the army a long time to resolve its problem of supplying such a large force in the field hundreds of miles from home. One of Bennington's wealthiest men, Trenor W. Park, who was living in California at the time, sent $1,000 to Governor Fairbanks to help supply the troops with the materials they needed for the defense of the country.

Trenor W. Park, circa 1850. *Bennington Museum, Bennington, Vermont.*

Recruiting continued in earnest. Lieutenant George Conkling opened a recruiting office in the Stark House on Main Street with plans to sign up a company of one hundred men for Ramsey's New York Regiment of light infantry. Everyone did what they could. F.C. White began collecting religious books to send to the men of the Second Vermont. When word came that the Second would pass through the North Bennington railroad depot on its way south, a thousand people turned out to cheer them on. On June 26, 1861, the regiment's train from Burlington stopped for about twenty minutes, and the townspeople passed cakes and pies through the open windows to the soldiers.[36]

In July 1861, another group of men calling themselves the Bennington Musketeers began drilling with Abraham B. Gardner as its captain.[37] By the end of that month, the Zouave Club had over fifty members and was reported to be the first Zouave company in the state. In August, when Ramsey's

Captain Abraham B. Gardner. *Bennington Museum, Bennington, Vermont.*

The juvenile Zouaves in Bennington. *Bennington Museum, Bennington, Vermont.*

Regiment was called up, they had managed to recruit only twenty-five men from Bennington, falling short of their goal of one hundred. That same month, Captain John E. Pratt began to recruit his own company of Zouaves from Bennington. Once organized, they would be mustered in as Company A of the Fourth Vermont Regiment. It became a fad for young boys to dress in Zouave colors and practice drilling with wooden rifles alongside the older men. The adults drilled for six hours each day and received "much praise for their fine appearance and soldierly bearing," said the editors of the *Banner.*[38]

During the summer of that first year of the war, the women of Bennington formed their own group called the Ladies' Soldiers' Aid Society. They elected Mrs. Caroline S. Hurlbut as their president and set about doing whatever

To the Ladies.

All those ladies who are willing to make any sacrifice in this hour of their country's peril, and are willing to come forth and pledge themselves for their country's good, not to use any imported article of apparel, are invited to meet at the rooms of the

Ladies' Soldiers' Aid Society, on Tuesday, May 17th, at 3 o'clock, P. M.

Bennington, May 13, 1864.

Ladies' Soldiers' Aid Society handbill, May 13, 1864. *Bennington Museum, Bennington, Vermont.*

they could to provide for the soldiers at the front.[39] They raised money and collected food, clothing and medical supplies, which were shipped off to various Vermont companies at regular intervals. Originally, the ladies met at the Franklin House, but eventually, they had their own office fitted up in a vacant storefront next to the post office.

Interest in the war grew with every new recruit, and people were eager to hear news from the front. An itinerant artist named Angell mounted a *Panorama of the War* one weekend. He rented the Apollo Hall for the exhibition, which centered on a giant mural-sized painting that depicted the early battles. His scroll picture was unfurled as Angell described each scene to the audience.[40] It must have been informative because the editors of the *Banner* declared that it was worth twice the price of admission. The following year, another panorama was offered by an artist named Williams. And then in 1864, the artists Lillie and Wilbur rented the same hall to show off their own panorama of the war. These traveling panoramas remained popular until the invention of the motion picture. In the fall of 1861, Governor Fairbanks set aside the last Thursday of September as a day for fasting, humiliation and prayer in support of the Union, and churches in Bennington held special services.

In October 1861, Captain Walbridge returned from the front lines to recruit new men for the Second Vermont Regiment. His mission was to restore

Officers of Company A, Second Vermont Regiment. *Bennington Museum, Bennington, Vermont.*

Company A to full strength after it had sustained losses. A Captain Duncan had been in town trying to raise enough men for a new company to be added to the Sixth Vermont Regiment, but when he failed to reach the needed goal of one hundred men, he disbanded the ones he had, and Captain Walbridge signed most of them on with the Second Vermont at twenty-dollars-per-month pay. The captain had seen action in the Battle of Bull Run, and during his visit to Bennington, he spoke to people in town about the grim realities of what now looked like it would be a much longer war. One thing that his men needed was boots because the ones that the army provided were not good for marching in wet weather, so the townspeople pulled together to raise money for those.[41]

The army was also busy buying local horses for use by the cavalry. It purchased many from Woodworth and West of Arlington, but after examination, between one-third and one-half of them were deemed unfit.[42] Already the war was bringing out the worst in some businessmen who saw the conflict as an opportunity to make a quick buck by selling inferior merchandise. These speculators and con artists were not unique to Bennington County, and across the country, similar problems were cropping up due to the enormous demands the army was making for war materials.

At 6:30 a.m. on Tuesday morning, October 15, 1861, everyone in town was awakened by an enormous explosion.[43] Two tons of gunpowder blew up at the Bennington Powder Works, whose mills were a few miles east of the center of town. The buildings were completely destroyed, and all the windows in the surrounding area were broken; but miraculously, no one was killed. Had the blast occurred just a few hours later, the area would have been filled with workmen, and the death toll would have been great. The Bennington Powder Works had been awarded a large government contract and was producing up to one thousand pounds of gunpowder a day. Undeterred, the company rebuilt quickly and continued to fill its contract. In June 1863, the company expanded and erected a new building for refining saltpeter, one of the ingredients used in the manufacture of gunpowder. Once again, disaster struck. On January 29, 1864, an even greater explosion wiped out five of its buildings. It was said to be the "most terrific powder mill explosion to ever occur in the area."[44] The company was again fortunate that the blast took place in the early morning hours and no deaths were reported, but still, the explosion could be felt up to one hundred miles away. Residents of Troy heard it, and Manchester's buildings shook. Although the roof was blown off the nearby powder magazine, the thirty thousand pounds of powder stored inside did not explode. In 1867, two years after the war, a third explosion occurred at the mill, which was located near where East Main Street intersects with the new bypass. This time, three men were killed, and although the company rebuilt, it closed for good a year or two later.

At the time of the first blast, Captain F.F. Streter was in town staying at the Franklin House recruiting men for the Third Company of Vermont Sharpshooters.[45] The requirements for that elite unit stated that a man had to be able to hit ten consecutive shots within a fifty-inch circle at a distance of two hundred yards. No one was able to qualify, and Streter left Bennington without any recruits at all. Although patriotism was still very high at this early point in the war, few people had the specialized skills needed by the army. Even the Mount Anthony Seminary students formed a company of militia under their captain, William Wilson, and began to drill two hours each day to prepare themselves for military service.[46]

On October 24, 1861, people in town were shocked to learn that Captain H.L. Shields of Troy, who had a summer residence just north of Bennington in a place known as "Furnace Grounds," had been arrested. Marshals came from Troy and sent a message to Captain Shields that a letter was waiting for him in the Arlington post office, and when he came down to retrieve it, he was arrested and taken away immediately.[47] He was transferred to

Captain H.L. Shields in his sleigh, painted by Thomas Van Zandt. *Bennington Museum, Bennington, Vermont.*

Fort Lafayette, the maximum-security prison in New York Harbor, and charged with treason for giving secret information to the enemy. Later, he was released when no evidence was found to back up the allegations.

During the fall of 1861, the people of Bennington carried on as best they could with so many of their young men going off to war. Dollie Dutton came to perform at Apollo Hall, much to the delight of the audience. She was a tiny woman, one-third the size of Tom Thumb, the showman P.T. Barnum's greatest attraction.[48] Lecturers, musicians and even phrenologists packed the auditorium for some diversionary entertainment during the long winter months. On the last Thursday of November, a day dedicated to giving thanks, many attended religious services to pray for the men away in the army. Eventually, this day of thought and reflection would become our Thanksgiving.

By the end of the year, the members of Bennington's band who had gone away to become the regimental band for the Second Vermont were mustered out and returned home. The government had been forced to cut the budget for musical bands; however, some of the men individually made arrangements to join other units where possible. Many townspeople turned out in the cold at the train depot to welcome them back.

1862

Throughout the war, the "Local Intelligence" column of the *Bennington Banner* was the main source for news of promotions, illnesses, furloughs and deaths among Bennington's soldiers. It charted the activities of many of the officers and some of the enlistees and noted when they were home on leave from their companies. From time to time, the newspaper would also make mention of the fact that officers' wives visited their husbands at the front, although usually when battles were imminent, they were sent home. The wives of Captains Pratt and Cady and Quartermaster Cushman were among those mentioned.

During 1862, the news from the front was not good. The Union troops had not gained much ground on the Confederate forces, and the war that had, at one time, seemed like it would be over within a few months was obviously going to drag on. Soldiers wrote home with discouraging news, and the local newspaper sometimes printed their letters from the front. Lieutenant Burton of Company A, Fourth Vermont Regiment, wrote about action taking place outside Richmond:

> *The line of our retreat was strewn with knapsacks, dead and wounded men, broken guns, wagons and all sorts of rations. We broke 8,000 new Enfield rifles at Savage Station, burnt up 1,300,000 rounds of cartridges, and any quantity of hard bread, pork and beef. I have been in three battles, and have come out all right, and can safely say I have caused more than one to bite the dust. I experienced a feeling of joy after the first fire, and was as cool as Greenland, but was quite excited at first.*[49]

Above: Battle between the *Monitor* and the *Merrimac. Print by John C. McRae, collection of the author.*

Right: John Winslow. *Vermont Historical Society.*

Charles Kelly, one of the soldiers in Captain Cady's company who was also at the Battle of Savage Station, said that he found a Rebel soldier, mortally wounded, who asked him to let his mother in South Carolina know of his death. Along with Kelly's letter, he sent home a small basket that he had found in a Rebel house whose occupants had fled from the battlefront.[50] These "secesh" mementoes often found their way back to Bennington homes during the war.

Grave of Private Edward Selden. *Author's collection.*

In the early spring of 1862, the people of Bennington heard about the March 8 and 9 naval battle between the *Monitor* and the *Merrimac*, but few knew that there was an unusual Bennington connection to that fight. John Winslow was born in Bennington in 1810. His father had a grocery business on Main Street, but the family appeared to have moved to Troy while he was still a boy. During the Civil War, Winslow and his business partner, John Griswold, worked with John Ericsson to construct the USS *Monitor*, the first boat to be designed as an ironclad warship. At the time, the navy didn't believe that ironclads would be effective, so it decided not to approve Ericsson's proposal, even though President Lincoln personally liked the idea. Griswold and Winslow met with Lincoln, and they decided to proceed with the project anyway, in spite of the navy's reluctance to fund it. Winslow financed the $275,000 construction project himself, and the boat was built in Brooklyn in 101 days. The *Monitor* was launched in 1862, just in time to do battle with the *Merrimac*, but since the navy had not paid for the ship, it was technically still Winslow's personal property. Immediately after the battle, however, the navy rushed to build dozens of ironclads and repaid Winslow for his investment.[51]

By 1862, bodies were beginning to be sent home. Captain Cady of the Second Vermont wrote of the death of Private Edward A. Selden of Bennington, whose body was being shipped back. "I am proud to say that he has been a splendid soldier, and done his duty like a man," Cady wrote.[52] Selden had been sick with dysentery for some time before his death, and they buried his body in the family plot at the Old Bennington Cemetery.

With metals of all sorts being in short supply, coins were becoming scarce, and the government passed a law to allow the use of postage stamps to replace coins from one to ninety cents. The merchants in town did an active business by trading stamps for merchandise. Still needing more troops in July 1862, President Lincoln called for another 300,000 volunteers. The people in Bennington responded quickly and held a meeting at Armory Hall on Saturday, July 19, 1862, for the purpose of complying with the president's request. That meeting was chaired by A.B. Gardner. At the suggestion of Hiland Hall, the meeting drafted a series of resolutions: 1) to support President Lincoln, 2) to approve his call for 300,000 volunteers and 3) to raise money for bounties of $50 each. At that meeting, they raised $750 for these bounties.[53]

The uniforms for Company E of the Tenth Vermont Regiment arrived in August and were fitted to the men. "The company looks finely in its new rig, and we think it is composed of as fine looking, hardy men as have left in any of the previous Companies," said the *Banner*. On August 12, 1862, after Reverend Phillips gave a sermon to the uniformed soldiers at the Methodist Church, Captain Madison Winslow marched his troops to the wagons of Norton and Sheldon, who took them over the mountains to the camp at Brattleboro. From there, the railroad would take them south. They left in "high spirits and with a full determination to do their part in crushing out the most wicked rebellion that ever disgraced the annals of any history," railed the editor of the *Banner*.[54]

Even as these men were being recruited and trained, a new call for additional troops had come. A Fourteenth Vermont Regiment was to be formed and Captain Ransom O. Gore was elected to lead Company A, composed of Bennington men. With him were First Lieutenant E.N. Thayer and Second Lieutenant Charles Albro, both of Bennington.[55] In September, the company took up residence in an empty building at the U.S. Pottery Works, and in no time, it had turned the place into a decent enough barracks. Regular drilling commenced under the tutelage of Cadet Gilbert D. Millington of Shaftsbury. He was appointed by Adjutant General Washburn for that position, and he set about putting the men through their paces for four or five hours each day. It took longer than expected to provide uniforms, however, because cloth was beginning to be scarce throughout the country. Thomas Keyes received the contract to make the uniforms for Captain Gore's company, and once he had the material in hand, it took him about a week to complete the work.[56]

While still in camp, the men of Company A presented a fine sword and scabbard to Lieutenant Albro. It was purchased by Mr. and Mrs. Marcius

Grave of Private Calvin Hathaway. *Author's collection.*

G. Selden as a sign of the high esteem they held for the young man. The presentation was made by Quartermaster John H. Cushman, who also gave him a handsomely bound copy of the Bible.[57] Just before the company left Brattleboro for the front, the men also presented Captain Gore with a fine sword and sash.[58] It was typical of troops to give presentation swords to their commanding officers throughout the war. These were ornately inscribed and were never used in battle but became treasured mementoes after the war. Several are to be found in the collection of the Bennington Museum.

Occasionally, there were reports of Bennington men being seen in the Confederate lines. Gordon E. Niles, once a resident of Bennington, was reported to have been killed with the Southern troops in the fighting around Gallatin, Kentucky. He was said to have joined the guerrilla band of raiders under General John Hunt Morgan and "fell fighting for treason," in the words of the *Bennington Banner*.[59] In September, it was reported that two Cushman boys, Frederick and Albert, were both active in the Rebel army. Fred served as quartermaster in the Tenth Georgia Regiment, and Albert participated in battles around Richmond as a member of the Eighth Georgia Regiment. It must have been very hard for their mother to see this mentioned in the local newspaper, especially when the same issue carried long casualty lists of Vermont soldiers killed and wounded at the Battles of Crampton Pass and Antietam.

Servicemen's bodies continued to be returned North whenever possible. In December, the body of seventeen-year-old Private Calvin Hathaway of Company A, Second Vermont Regiment, arrived at the train station and was greeted by a large number of mourners who included Calvin's Sunday school classmates. They accompanied his casket to the cemetery and said prayers as he was lowered into the ground. It was noted that while he was in the hospital in Hagerstown, Maryland, Mrs. C.S. Canfield of New Jersey, visiting her own wounded son in the same hospital, had realized that Private Hathaway didn't have long to live. She kindly stayed until the end, talking and praying with him. Joseph H. Loring was hired by the Hathaway family of Bennington to go south and bring home Private Hathaway's body. This was not uncommon during the Civil War, and people often went to the battlefield to try to locate wounded or dead relatives and friends. On the same trip, Mr. Loring was unable to find the remains of Henry Loveland of Company A, Fourth Vermont Regiment to return to his widowed mother, Mrs. Silvia Loveland of Bennington.[60] The above information from the newspaper at the time is a bit of a mystery because more recent documentation shows that Hathaway is now buried at the National Cemetery in Antietam, and a cenotaph to his memory is in the Village Cemetery here, while Loveland's body is actually buried in the Village Cemetery.

In addition to the bodies of the dead, men who had been wounded were beginning to arrive home too. One soldier, Sergeant F.P. Aylesworth of Manchester lost one of his legs and the toes of his other foot due to the carelessness and inattention of hospital surgeons. The *Banner* scolded, "O, for shame on such treatment of our brave young men who have thus periled life and limb for the salvation of our country!" Once home, Sergeant Aylesworth learned the art of ornamental hair design. That was a craft that used braided human hair to make wreaths and jewelry, both popular art forms at the time. The *Banner* urged people to make use of his services and help him earn a living through his craft.[61]

Not everyone who went to the battlefield was in the military. Members of the Riddell family of Bennington were active on the front lines as merchants doing business with the soldiers in their camps. They were called sutlers, and they sold various goods to the troops, anything from bread and clothing to needles and thread could be obtained for a price. In January and February, there were mentions of various members of the Riddell family in the newspaper. It seems that one of the Riddell brothers, Samuel, was taken prisoner by the Rebels at St. Augustine, Florida. He and about twenty-five other men were ambushed and captured, and although they were not soldiers, they were held as prisoners by the Confederates.[62]

1863

During the winter of 1862–63, many festivals and dances were held at Apollo Hall and other venues around town for the benefit of sick and wounded soldiers, raising several hundred dollars from these events. The Ladies' Soldiers' Aid Society continued to hold gatherings to raise money for the packages they were sending to the troops. The newspapers frequently listed the contents of the boxes sent. An example of the contents of one box was "one bottle strawberries, two dozen raspberries, six dozen whortleberries, eight dozen shrub, thirteen dozen currant wine, one dozen raspberry wine, one dozen brandy, six dozen crab apple jelly, one dozen currant jelly, one dozen currants, six dozen tomatoes, one jar currants, one jar currant jelly, one bottle currant and raspberry jelly, one box mustard."[63]

In addition to the stories about the bravery and valor of the Bennington troops, there were other stories that showed another side of the war. Early in 1863, Colonel Charles Carroll Hicks, a soldier in the Confederate army, was arrested in New York City as a spy and imprisoned at Fort Lafayette. Colonel Hicks was the husband of Sophia A. Hicks, who had been a resident of Bennington up until her death on February 3, 1863. Sophia was the daughter of John Cushman. In 1861, Charles, the suspected spy, had given a lecture in Bennington on the subject of Garibaldi that had been praised by the *Banner* at the time. Now the paper called him "an undoubted traveling specimen of unadulterated rascality."[64]

As an active railroad center, many trains passed through North Bennington on their way to the front. On May 18, 1863, an enormous gun passed

Rodman gun similar to the one that passed through North Bennington. *Author's collection.*

through town on its way from the Fort Pitt foundry in Pittsburgh to Boston, where a gunboat was being prepared for it. A huge crowd of people turned out to inspect the fifteen-inch-bore Rodman gun that weighed all of 42,500 pounds, one of the largest guns to ever be put on board a boat. It would have had a range of nearly five thousand yards and shot a cannonball weighing 400 pounds. "An engine of death and destruction to the rebels," the editor of the *Banner* stated.[65] It is amazing how much military information about weapons and troop movements appeared in local papers at that time. Not all facts were true, however. Rumors were widespread and often repeated. In May 1863, the *Troy Whip* reported that Richmond had fallen and that Lee was in retreat. This was just before the decisive battle at Gettysburg. Other false rumors that circulated included news that an entire Vermont regiment had been captured by the enemy.

Canada became a frequent destination for army deserters, but in the summer of 1863 the Canadian government agreed to return all legitimate deserters and draft dodgers. The *Bennington Banner* reported that "quite a number who enlisted from this town are supposed to be there."[66] In July

1863, three deserters were captured locally. Deputy Provost Marshal Viall, assisted by Lieutenant D.M. Blackmer, caught Warren Dutcher, L. Towslee and a Mr. Powers, all men from the area, who had each enlisted several times only to desert after receiving their bounties. The problems of enlistments and desertions became even bigger that month as the government took steps to enforce a draft that proved very unpopular with the people. Bennington was still doing pretty well enlisting volunteers, but they had to raise the bounty for new recruits from $50 to $300. By doing so, the town fathers felt that they would have enough men to fill the quota and the draft would not be necessary. Before the end of the war, the bounty would be raised again to $450 and, finally, to $700, a sizeable nest egg in those days for anyone who agreed to join the army. A list of the men drafted that summer appeared in the newspaper. Of those, four paid for their replacements, one man was not an American and three men were rejected due to physical disabilities. A Bennington man named Edward Ray, who was a member of the New Lebanon Shakers, was drafted into a New York regiment, but he was rejected due to a defect in his fingers. In response to the new draft law, a group of Shaker elders went to secure an exemption from military service since the Shakers were pledged never to harm another person. Lincoln granted them the status of conscientious objectors on religious grounds, one of the first such exemptions in history.

The state continued to think of ways to get more recruits, and money seemed like the only thing that really worked. An advertisement appeared in the press that said, "Enlist! Enlist! This State now pays $654.00 for Old Veterans, and $554.00 for fresh recruits. What business pays better? Rally, then, and fill up the Regiments. The government wants men now, not next year—the war will undoubtedly be at an end then."[67]

As a result of the draft, another interesting organization was created at this time. A group of six young men from Bennington formed a Mutual Insurance Company to pay their commutation money in the event that they were drafted. When two of their members were selected in the draft, each of the men paid in $100 for William H. Grover and George H. Day, the two draftees. They were then able to pay off their $300 bounty for replacements.[68] Surprisingly, not even freed slaves were exempt from the draft. Stephen Adams, whose name appears among the drafted men from Bennington, was listed as a "contraband," meaning that he had been freed by the Union army from his masters in the South and allowed to relocate to the North. He was liberated by the Reverend Asher Prentiss, whose mother was living in Bennington Center and Adams had come here to work for Mrs. Prentiss.[69] Four months later, he was drafted. Townspeople worked to secure an exemption for the former slave, as it would be dangerous for him to return to the South. They must have been successful because his name does not appear on the roster of Vermont veterans.

The issue of what to do with former slaves was an important one. In Bennington, it was a topic of much conversation, and Reverend Whittemore, an agent of the Freedmen's Association, addressed a large audience at the Congregational Church on behalf of the cause. He showed photographs of former slaves now under the protection of the Freedmen's Association and asked for donations to help relocate ex-slaves.[70]

Captain Gore's Company A of the Fourteenth Vermont Regiment was composed of men who had only volunteered for a nine-month tour of duty, but still they managed to see action in early July 1863 at Gettysburg. They suffered casualties, including William Reay and James Grace of Bennington, who were listed among the wounded. The company was mustered out on July 21, and a grand celebration to welcome it home was planned. Before that happened, the people of Bennington received the welcome news that Major General George Gordon Meade had triumphed over General Robert E. Lee at Gettysburg. Two hundred guns were fired in the village; people rejoiced and were hopeful that the end was now in sight and that all their boys would soon be home. Such was not to be, however. President Lincoln called for a national day of Thanksgiving to be held on August 6, 1863. There were appropriate services held at all the churches in town, with some of the ministers trading parishes for the occasion. On the evening of August 15, in honor of Bennington Battle Day, fireworks, furnished by Seth B. Hunt, were set off from the top of Bald Mountain. The fifty or sixty rockets were to honor General Grant for his victory at Vicksburg and General Meade for his at Gettysburg, but the war was only half over.[71]

During the Battle of Gettysburg, one Wilmington, Vermont man managed to escape from the Rebel army and make his way to the Union lines, where he surrendered. He said he had been in the South at the outbreak of war and was pressed into service there against his will. Gettysburg had been his first chance to desert. He had been an unwilling soldier throughout but was obliged, like thousands of others, the *Bennington Banner* said, "to make a virtue of necessity, keeping an eye open all the while for a chance to get away."[72]

In September 1863, the newspaper reported that Mrs. Mary Todd Lincoln and her son Tad, along with Major General Abner Doubleday and his wife, had passed through North Bennington on the train.[73] They had just spent a few weeks at the Equinox House in Manchester and enjoyed it so much that they planned to repeat the trip the following summer. Years later, the Lincolns' other

Mary Todd Lincoln. *Author's collection.*

son, Robert Todd Lincoln, was to build Hildene as his own summer home in Manchester.

That fall, another call was made by President Lincoln for an additional 300,000 troops, and so once again, the town met, this time on November 24, 1863, in the courthouse, to decide how to handle the new request. Again, they voted to pay the bounties of each town resident drafted. Bennington's full quota to be raised was 65 men, but due to existing volunteers, they had credit and needed to find only 29 more men to reach the goal.[74] Surrounding towns were all in the same position, and by now, they were competing for volunteers; so the towns that paid the most were the most likely to meet their quotas before the actual draft took place. In this area, the towns tried to agree beforehand to limit the bounties to $200 per man, but in Boston, the bounties were reaching $450 in some cases. In an effort to compete, local towns began to break their pledges to keep the fee fixed at $200, and the Bennington town fathers met at Apollo Hall, where they voted to raise their bounty to $300 for that reason. At that meeting, Colonel Randall spoke to those assembled. He acknowledged that many people in the North were discouraged because the rebellion was not put down in the first thirty days of the war. Randall went on to say that three-fourths of the Fifth Vermont Regiment had reenlisted when their terms had expired and he believed the numbers would be the same for the Third and Fourth Vermont Regiments, too. If they did reenlist, the Bennington members of the Fourth Vermont would be home on a thirty-day furlough before their next three years' enlistment period began. By the end of the year, Bennington was only two men short of meeting its quota.

1864

The war proved to be good business, and area industrialists were prospering because of it. R. Carpenter Jr. and Company in North Bennington received a contract from the government to manufacture 150,000 yards of army cloth, and more orders were promised. Henry Burden, the owner of the famous ironworks in Troy, also had extensive operations in both Bennington and Shaftsbury. He had the patent on a horseshoe-making machine that was used exclusively by the army, and it netted him giant profits. Locally, he expanded his iron furnace operations to accommodate the increased volume of business and employed more than fifty men in Bennington County. Even men like Calvin Dart, who ran an Ambrotype Saloon on the second floor of the building at the corner of Main and North Streets, did well taking photographs of soldiers in their new uniforms.[75] These became cherished possessions of their families and loved ones. And although the tourist business suffered throughout the war, places like Gates Hotel were able to make up lost revenues by renting out rooms to the state government to be used by men who were training for military service.

Olin Scott, one of the town's most successful businessmen, also profited from the war effort. He produced all of the machinery used to make gunpowder in America. He was truly a self-made man and bought mills in downtown Bennington for his foundry business. Early in 1864, he purchased real estate at the head of Pleasant Street and built several buildings there, consolidating his business. Then he put up an elegant house for himself next door to the factory. He was close to the stream, so he had abundant water

Left: Olin Scott. *Author's collection.*

Below: National Bank of North Bennington. *Author's collection.*

power, which he put to good use. Some of his buildings, as well as his home, are still standing today, and the Olin Scott Foundation, which he created, still offers low-interest loans to area students.

The town also received a shot in the arm from the federal government during the Civil War in the form of new banks. Both Bennington and North

Bennington established national banks as a result of legislation passed in 1863 and 1864. It was then that the U.S. government established a system of national banks created to encourage the development of a national currency backed by U.S. Treasury securities. The government was spending so much money on the war effort that it was running out of gold and silver, so it began to issue paper money in lieu of coins. This act established the banking and monetary system that we still use today. The quantity of notes that a bank was allowed to issue was proportional to the bank's level of capital deposited with the U.S. Treasury. In effect, these laws took banking out of the hands of state governments. Trenor W. Park and his partners put up capital amounting to $400,000 to set up the "First National Bank in North Bennington" and then engaged an architect to design the brick bank building that still stands in the center of the village today.[76] Within a few months, it had become the largest banking institution in the state. At the same time, Henry Root and Luther Graves, local merchants of tin ware and glassware, established the First National Bank of Bennington. Originally, they had offices in a room in the building next to the post office, and in 1868, they built the beautiful brick building still standing at 332 Main Street, where the bank remained

Bennington Free Library. *Author's collection.*

until 1931. Without the monetary crisis caused by the Civil War, these banks would not have existed.

Trenor Park also teamed up with Seth Hunt in 1864 to purchase the Wheeler Building, and on its site they put up a public library, which still stands today at the corner of Main and Silver Streets.[77] The building was designed with a public hall on the upper floor at a cost of approximately $10,000. As soon as it opened, the library hall became the venue for many important town meetings and lectures.

When another call came from President Lincoln for more troops, the town met and decided once again to raise the bounty, this time to $700 for new recruits. When the question of bounties for reenlisting soldiers arose, it was quickly agreed that they should be awarded the same amount. As a result, nineteen members of Company A, Fourth Vermont Regiment, and twenty members of Company G, First Vermont Cavalry, reenlisted when their terms of duty expired. A few young Bennington lads decided to enlist in the navy instead of the army. One such volunteer, John Leonard, enlisted in 1863 and served on the USS *Neptune*.[78] The *Neptune* was a large, wooden steamer that served as an escort vessel in the West Indies, using its powerful guns to protect commercial ships on their way back from California.

Not all volunteers were successful in the army for a variety of reasons. Everett Joy, who enlisted from Bennington, was quickly sent home when it was found that he was too young to serve, and the *Banner* noted that he was "not possessing quite back bone enough to endure the hardship of camp life."[79] In April 1864, Company F of the Seventeenth Vermont Regiment was formed. It became the last Bennington unit to be created during the war, although other individuals were recruited for existing units until the end of the fighting. Company F selected Captain Lyman E. Knapp of Townshend to lead them, but his first lieutenant would be George Hicks and his third sergeant, Samuel B. Norton, both of Bennington. The editor of the newspaper summed up the town's feelings when he wrote:

> *It is a source of pride and congratulation to us, as we doubt not it is to every citizen of our County, to know that gloriously and unflinchingly as Vermont has come up to the work of sustaining the Government, and furnishing bone and sinew for its army, Bennington County has the honor of having furnished more men, in proportion to its size, and the number of its able-bodied citizens, than any other County in the State. This is a flattering record, and one which the Southern extremity of the old Green Mountain State has a right to be proud of.*[80]

In April 1864, Colonel J.H. Walbridge resigned his commission with the "bully old 2nd" as the Second Vermont had become known. The colonel was in continued bad health, and his physicians feared that he would not recover if he remained in the service. Under his leadership, the regiment had undergone some of its severest tests and gained many of its highest honors. Colonel Walbridge was succeeded by Lieutenant Colonel Newton Stone, who had originally entered the service as a lieutenant in Company A of the Second Vermont. Within weeks of his appointment, however, Colonel Stone was killed in action. Stone was the son of a Readsboro minister and had joined the army at the age of twenty-three, shortly after he had been admitted to the bar. On the second day of the Battle of the Wilderness in May of that year, he was struck in the leg and rushed back to the aid station. There, they dressed his wound, and he rode back to the line and into the thick of the fighting. When his men saw him, they greeted him with a cheer, but almost immediately, he was struck in the head with a bullet and died instantly.

Ministers from various churches in Bennington made their way to the battlefields, too. The Reverend William Stokes Apsey, minister of the First Baptist church from 1862 to 1868, volunteered to attend to sick and wounded soldiers for a few weeks, while working with the Christian Commission in Virginia.[81] Other ministers performed similar duties throughout the course of the war.

Throughout 1864, it must have seemed like the war would never end. The newspaper alternated stories about the war with local interest items, maybe hoping to soften the blow of too many casualty lists. These items appeared side by side in the "Local Intelligence" column of the *Banner*:

> *Fishing—Trout fishing on the mountains is fast getting to be in its prime, and numbers of our fishermen daily hie them thereto, and return well repaid for their labors. Our "city cousins" will do well to be here soon to take a hand in.*
>
> *Wounded and Taken Prisoner—Lucias K. Billings, who formerly resided here, being in the employ of Messrs. Graves & Root, was severely, and it is feared, according to reports, mortally wounded, in the great battle of the 6th and taken prisoner. He belonged to a New York Regiment.*
>
> *More Men To Be Needed. It seems that a new call up of men will come soon and the editors want the town to arrange for the bounties and recruit men before the draft.*[82]

General George B. McClellan. *Author's collection.*

By June, the country was beginning to think about the upcoming presidential election to be held the following November. It was by no means certain that Abraham Lincoln would be reelected. In fact, later that summer, when the popular General George B. McClellan decided to throw his hat into the ring, it looked like Lincoln might be a one-term president. Bennington's A.B. Gardner and A.M. Huling were chosen to represent Vermont at the party convention that would nominate Lincoln.

In August, the newspaper put out a call for new recruits:

> *"Rally Around the Flag, Boys, Rally Once Again!"—To those desirous of entering the army, we can confidently assure that a more favorable opportunity than is now presented, will not offer itself during the war. Larger bounties are now being paid than we believe will ever be paid again. The Selectmen of Bennington are now paying $700.00 for three years' volunteers, and with this liberal bounty, coupled with that paid by the General Government, it does seem as though our quota would be filled at once. There remains yet one month before the draft, and let all take hold of the business of recruiting in good earnest, and the full number required of this town and County will be obtained.*[83]

The president's new call would be for a half million troops, and Bennington's share would probably be around four hundred men this time. The increased bounty quickly brought in about one-third of the necessary number, so they were well on their way. H.D. Hall and Elijah Dewey both hired substitutes and received exemption papers for three years, and Henry F. Dewey went off to other towns to procure substitutes for a club of ten men who had pooled their resources. By the time the draft was held in late September, all the necessary substitutes had been found, and Bennington's quota was filled; so no one was forced to serve through conscription.

During the later part of the summer of 1864, a shoddy manufactory was started in the unoccupied pottery buildings on North Street that were owned by Enos Adams and Company.[84] In the 1840s, Reuben Daniels of Woodstock, Vermont, had invented a machine to make a type of cloth that was called shoddy. The material was made from reprocessed wool and rags and it resembled felt. During the Civil War, the Union army hired a clothing manufacturer in New York City by the name of Brooks Brothers to make uniforms for the soldiers. The war had created such an enormous demand for wool that when Brooks Brothers couldn't get enough woolen material, it decided to use shoddy cloth, a short-fibered version made from scraps.

Brooks Brothers made a fortune, but before long, the troops discovered that uniforms made of this material didn't hold up in the rain—the cloth literally fell apart. Thus, "shoddy" came to represent an inferior-quality product, and the name has stuck ever since. There is no evidence that the shoddy manufactured in Bennington was ever used for uniforms, however. Even though shoddy was proven inadequate for clothing, it had other uses and was still in demand.

After the initial call-up for three-month men in 1861, most of the volunteers had enlisted for three years, so by the late summer of 1864, the town began to see returning veterans. In September, forty-five of the original members of the Fifth Vermont Regiment who had not reenlisted passed through town on their way to Burlington, where the were to be mustered out. Captain Cady returned home from his three-year term of duty and partnered with J.S. Carpenter in running a saloon and billiard room downtown. It became a popular place for returning veterans to meet and talk over their experiences. In October 1864, the topic of conversation must have turned to George Benjamin, a native of Bennington and a former member of Company A, Second Vermont Regiment.[85] He had turned up alive in Canada. This was surprising because a year and a half earlier he had been reported as dead. His death turned out to be a hoax that he had perpetrated in order to cover his desertion from the regiment. He had been holed up with a dying man in a shack somewhere in Virginia, and when the man passed away, it occurred to Benjamin that he could plant his own identification on the dead man's body and no one would be the wiser. His relatives mourned his passing, and his estate was settled, while Benjamin himself hid out in Canada. It wasn't until a fellow Benningtonian happened to bump into him on a Canadian street that the true story became known.

As the day for the 1864 presidential election neared, Union troops under both General Grant and General Sherman made significant advances on Richmond and Atlanta. Those advances more than anything else helped swing the vote to Lincoln. On November 8, he and vice-presidential candidate Andrew Johnson won a clear victory over General McClellan. In Bennington, it was a landslide with 463 votes cast for Lincoln against 236 for McClellan. Abe's victory gave the town something to celebrate. Patriotic speeches were made, and an illumination was presented throughout the village. In those preelectric days, an illumination was a festive event in which businesses and homes were lit up after dark by lanterns that predated modern spotlights. All the businesses around the Four Corners, as well as the Mount Anthony Seminary in Old Bennington, were brightly lit in honor of the Republican victory.[86]

People in town were disturbed by the reports of the terrible conditions in Southern prisons like Libby and Andersonville, since many local soldiers were imprisoned there. Sergeant W.A. Comar of Bennington, a member of Company A of the Fourth Vermont Regiment, died in Andersonville under the cruelest of circumstances. He was sick with an untreated kidney disease for two weeks before he finally passed away from lack of food, clean water and medical treatment. This news was related by an escaped prisoner who managed to make his way back to the Union lines from the prison in central Georgia. Lewis Knapp, another local man, had also died in the same prison camp just before the escape. Like many soldiers, Knapp was survived by a widow and children who were left to fend for themselves.

Major Pratt himself had been captured and was rumored to be in Libby Prison in Richmond, another terrible hell-hole nearly as bad as Andersonville, but it was later learned that he was in a prison near Charleston, South Carolina, and receiving much better treatment due to his rank. Many prisoners were swapped in prisoner exchanges or released on parole. Most eventually went back to their regiments to fight again. Charles Johnson and Moses Smith, both of Bennington's Company A of the Fourth Vermont Regiment, returned from Southern prisons on parole. Both "showed signs of the grossest treatment at the hand of the rebel 'chivalry,' being very much emaciated, and were truly pitiable," said the *Banner*.[87] Although the South was accused of having the most inhumane prisons, more recent evidence points out that Northern prisoner of war camps, such as the one in Elmira, New York, were not much better.

1865

At Last the War Is Over

When Captains Gore's and Cady's enlistments were up, they returned to Bennington. Although they were no longer under army orders, they helped organize two companies of militia in Bennington and Woodford. They were appointed by Superintendent Charles Field to raise troops under a new military law. These troops were to act only as reserve forces, but members were required to drill frequently and prepare for combat if needed. In Bennington, they managed to fill their quotas in the time allotted, but fortunately, the men were never called into active duty.[88]

On April 6, 1865, the *Bennington Banner* announced that Richmond had fallen. A few days earlier, the Confederate troops had retreated, and Union forces, led by a troop of African American soldiers, had marched through the streets of the Rebel capital and taken control of the city. Under the command of General Ripley of Rutland, the Union soldiers opened the doors of Libby Prison and freed the Northern soldiers who were starving to death inside. The key to the prison was brought back to Vermont by the general as a souvenir and is today with the rest of his Civil War memorabilia in the Bennington Museum.

Seth B. Hunt, the wealthy businessman whose summerhouse was called Maple Grove and is currently the building that houses the administrative offices of the Soldiers' Home of Vermont, had promised to roast an ox when Richmond capitulated, and he kept his word. Although he was not able to come to Bennington to do it himself due to a sickness in his family, he sent word instructing Judge B.R. Sears exactly how to carry out his promise. A 1,600-pound ox was butchered and packages of 10 pounds each were given away to the needy in town.[89]

On April 9, 1865, Lee surrendered at Appomattox, Virginia. The end of the long war had finally arrived. In Bennington, church bells rang for two or three hours at a time. That was interspersed with the firing of a cannon that continued well into the night. In the evening, a giant illumination took place around the Four Corners area, and people cheered and celebrated wildly. Tongue-in-cheek, the *Banner* reported: "Casualties—A noted copperhead [a Northerner who was pro-South], residing in Shaftsbury, on reading the news fell backwards upon the ground, and to all appearances instantly expired. A neighbor of his, of the same stripe, was so affected by the news and the fate of his friend, that he became at once hopelessly insane."[90]

General Edward H. Ripley. *Bennington Museum, Bennington, Vermont.*

Within a week, all these happy festivities came to an abrupt halt when news reached town that President Lincoln had been assassinated in Washington on April 15, 1865. A few days later, on April 19, a standing-room-only crowd of mourners packed the new Free Library Hall (which had only been dedicated a month earlier) to hear a memorial service in honor of the slain president. All the speakers lamented his loss to the nation and prayed that his soul would be at peace in heaven. The proceedings were marked with great solemnity and deep sorrow. The members of both the Protection and Spartan Fire Engine Companies attended in full uniform. The courthouse, still at Bennington Center near the Old First Congregational Church, was tastefully draped in black, and the old silk flag bequeathed to the town by Governor Isaac Tichnor was displayed. The Reverend Isaac Jennings of Old First offered appropriate somber remarks. The choir sang, and guns were fired at regular intervals throughout the day.[91] That Sunday, all the churches in the village offered prayer and memorial services. Most of the buildings in town were draped in

THE OBSEQUIES OF ABRAHAM LINCOLN.
W.W.

Reverend Isaac Jennings standing at the pulpit of the First Congregational Church. *Bennington Museum, Bennington, Vermont.*

Opposite: The Obsequies of Abraham Lincoln memorial pamphlet. *Author's collection.*

black mourning cloths, the shops of E. Spiegel, G.B. Sibley, T.J. Tiffany, J.T. Shurtleff and S.F. Harris being the most conspicuous. Thatcher and Cady's storefront was decorated in a similar fashion with a motto commemorating the sad occasion. Later, a memorial fund was established, and gifts for the late president's family were collected at the post office.

In keeping with the grief-stricken times, the body of Bennington's Colonel Newton Stone was returned from the battlefield cemetery on June 6 and carried

General Joseph Hooker. *Author's collection.*

to the Old Bennington Cemetery's vault. He was interred on June 22 after his body had lain in state in the courthouse.[92] His coffin was draped with the grand old flag that the ladies had made for "the Bennington Boys" only four years earlier. Sympathizing friends threw bouquets of flowers into the open grave, and finally, the war seemed to be put to rest.

In conjunction with the Bennington Battle Day celebrations that year, an enormous welcome home for the troops was announced for August 16, 1865. The committee of arrangements was headed by Major General George J. Stannard, General T.O. Seaver and Brigadier General George P. Foster. That day was to be the grandest Battle Day on record with between ten and fifteen thousand people in attendance. The midday parade began at the Mount Anthony House and proceeded to a picnic grove on the eastern end of town. There, General "Fighting Joe" Hooker made a few remarks and ex-Governor Hiland Hall introduced the keynote speaker, Reverend Edwin Hubbell Chapin, one of the great orators of the day. One of the defenders of Fort Sumter, General Truman Seymour, a native of Vermont, was on hand and spoke briefly, as did Major General Carr of Troy and Major General Stannard, who had come home after the Battle of the Wilderness minus his right arm. The evening concluded with a wonderful fireworks display and a military ball held in the Free Library Hall. It was the last time that many of the officers would wear their uniforms.[93]

Postscript

There is another Bennington story with a Civil War connection that is little known today but illustrates the bitter feelings that lingered after the war was over. Most of us know that Abraham Lincoln's wife, Mary Todd Lincoln, spent two of her summers as first lady vacationing at the Equinox Inn in Manchester, Vermont. But you might be surprised to learn that the first lady of the Confederacy, Mrs. Jefferson Davis, visited Bennington, too. Following the surrender at Appomattox, the Confederate ex-president, Jefferson Davis, was charged with treason and held in prison at Fort Monroe for nearly two years before being released on $100,000 bail. While he awaited trial, he was permitted to live in Canada with his wife, Varina, their children and Varina's mother, Mrs. Margaret Howell. In October 1867, Mrs. Howell left Canada and came to Bennington to visit the family of industrialist Henry W. Patchin in Bennington Centre.[94] While here, Mrs. Howell became seriously ill, and her daughter, Mrs. Jefferson Davis, came down to care for her and take her back to Canada. Mrs. Howell died in Montreal just a few days after they returned. One book even claimed that the mother-in-law died in Bennington, but that seems to be incorrect because she is buried in Montreal. In Mrs. Davis's autobiography, she wrote, "In Bennington I had additional proof of how far party and sectional rancor could carry people, and how pitiless they become."

She wrote that in response to an editorial that appeared in the *Bennington Banner* on November 7, 1867. The newspaper pointed out that letters were passing through the Bennington Post Office addressed to the Honorable

Jefferson Davis—those would probably have been letters written by Varina Davis to her husband in Canada. The editorial said, "Honorable, indeed! What is it this man has done—the most infamous traitor in all the passage of time, to make him honorable?"[95]

Part II

Guide to Bennington's Civil War Sites

Old Bennington

William Lloyd Garrison Memorial

This memorial is located on the Old Bennington Village Green, and it is perhaps the best place to begin a tour of Bennington's Civil War sites. The memorial was erected one hundred years ago in William Lloyd Garrison's memory. For less than a year, from October 1828 until March 1829, Garrison (1805–1879) worked in Bennington as the editor of a newspaper named the *Journal of the Times*. It had a circulation of about six hundred and was published in an office that stood not far from today's monument. Early references say that the printing shop was on the grounds of the old Swift home next to the village school playground. That would place it somewhere in front of the houses facing the monument.

William Lloyd Garrison was a central figure in the early abolitionist movement in America. Most agree that it was the fear of abolition that eventually pushed the South to war. Vermont historian Howard Coffin suggests that the very beginnings of the Civil War could be traced to Garrison's arrival in Bennington. It was here that he first began to make a name for himself as an outspoken newspaperman and orator. Garrison had been hired by a group of Bennington's townsmen to establish a newspaper with several goals in mind. The first was to defeat Andrew Jackson in his bid for the presidency. They wanted a newspaper that would back President John Quincy Adams, who was running for reelection. However, Jackson won the election and became our seventh president. The owners of the newspaper

William Lloyd Garrison Monument. *Author's collection.*

were also active in the temperance movement and wanted a newspaper that supported their position. Most of all, they wanted a newspaper that would be an advocate in the fight to end slavery nationwide. Due to the efforts of people such as Garrison, the abolitionist movement grew in the Northern states, and by 1846, it was estimated that nearly 80 percent of Vermonters opposed slavery. After working on the Bennington newspaper for less than a year, Garrison went on to found the *Liberator* in Baltimore. It became the most influential abolitionist publication during the antebellum era.

The bronze relief on the memorial shows an early Franklin Printing Press, much like the one that Garrison would have used in his shop here. The monument was erected with donations from local townspeople, as well as wealthy summer visitors from Troy. Even Andrew Carnegie was listed among the donors.

OLD BENNINGTON ACADEMY BUILDING

30 Monument Avenue

This Federal-style brick school building shows Dutch influences and was built in 1821, as the oval stone tablet under the peak indicates. Originally, the first floor was a common school and the second floor was the academy (or high

Old Bennington Academy building. *Author's collection.*

school) where advanced students studied Latin and Greek in preparation for college and careers as lawyers or ministers. In 1829, William Lloyd Garrison gave one of his earliest antislavery lectures in this building. It is believed that fewer than a dozen people were in attendance. The opposition newspaper was critical of Garrison and his politics, calling him "Lord Garrulous." They reported that only one person attended his talk and that he had to be paid to do so.

UEL ROBINSON HOUSE

18 Monument Avenue

Both Charles and Frederick Robinson were born and raised on Monument Avenue in this 1828 clapboard house, the home of their father, Uel Robinson, just as it says on the historical marker. Like other boys their age, the Robinson boys enlisted in the army when war broke out. Charles was in his late twenties, and Frederick was just eighteen at the time. What makes their story unusual for Bennington is that they enlisted in the North Carolina Infantry and fought for the Confederacy.

The older brother, Charles, was a businessman who had married into a North Carolina family and was already settled in the South in 1861. When the fighting began, his younger brother joined him in North Carolina. The brothers took part in many battles until they were both taken prisoner at the Battle of Bentonville, North Carolina, in March 1865, very near the end of the war. Bentonville was the final clash between the armies of Major General William Sherman and General Joseph Johnston. The following month, after General Lee conceded defeat, General Johnston surrendered his army, effectively ending the war. Following the Civil War, the Robinson brothers stayed in North Carolina. Frederick married a local girl and worked as a grocery clerk until his death. The two brothers are buried in a North Carolina cemetery. This is a good example of what is meant when they say this was a war that divided families because many of the other Robinson boys fought on the side of the Union.

MOUNT ANTHONY SEMINARY

Seminary Lane

In 1829, when James Ballard, the headmaster of the Bennington Academy, was fired from that school on Monument Avenue for political reasons, he established the Bennington Seminary, later to be called the Mount Anthony Seminary. A supporter of his, Dr. Herman Swift, donated the land for the school, and they quickly erected the building, which still stands. During the Civil War, it was reported that some Southern sympathizers in Bennington planned to burn down the offices of the *Bennington Banner*, the home of Marshall Carter Hall (Hiland Hall's son) and the seminary. When one of the professors from the school, George W. Yates, heard that story, he went to Williamstown, borrowed twenty old muzzleloading rifles from the Williams College militia and brought them back to Bennington.[96] The rumor proved to be false, and the students did not have to use force to defend their school. It was also reported in the *Banner* that one of the students from the seminary left to join the Thirty-fifth Alabama Regiment, but the newspaper didn't identify the student. Supposedly, he was killed at the Battle of Nashville fighting with General Hood. Two other students joined Northern regiments and survived the war.[97]

OLD BENNINGTON CEMETERY

Monument Avenue next to the Old First Congregational Church

Before looking at Bennington's cemeteries, it should be mentioned that many of the men killed in action during the Civil War were buried on the battlefield. Sometimes their bodies could not be identified, and many times their remains could not be sent back immediately. If they died in Southern prisons, they were often buried in mass graves. It took weeks or even months to retrieve bodies from Southern battlefields, and it was expensive to do so. Occasionally, families sent someone South to retrieve the remains, but that was often the exception. For that reason it is unusual to see graves for men actually killed in action this far North, although Bennington has a few. Sometimes cenotaphs appear in family plots. These are markers that look like headstones but actually are memorials to the men who are buried elsewhere. And it should be mentioned that there are hundreds and hundreds of Civil War graves in Bennington, far too many to list in this book. The following is merely a selection of graves aimed at highlighting a wide variety of interesting stories. People who were demoted, deserted or did not serve are noted because they are also a part of the Civil War story. The Old Bennington Cemetery contains the graves of more than fifty Civil War soldiers.

Norman Puffer's Grave

There is always uncertainty when it comes to identifying the youngest or oldest soldier in any war, but if Norman Martin Puffer (1847–1912) was not the youngest from Vermont, he was at least the second youngest. Recently, another soldier has been discovered who may have been a few days younger than Puffer, who was only fourteen when he enlisted in June 1861. He became the drummer boy, first for the Second Vermont Infantry Band and later for the Tenth Vermont Infantry. He served throughout the duration of

Second Vermont regimental band with Norman Puffer standing on the left, December 11, 1861. *Bennington Museum, Bennington, Vermont.*

the war, and when peace came, he had not yet turned eighteen. His older brothers, Wales and Alfred, also served in the Union army.[98]

This little drummer boy was born in Bennington and grew up to become one of its most prominent and successful citizens before he passed away in 1912 at his home on Union Street. A family genealogy says that Norman was present at Lee's surrender to Grant at Appomattox and that he took part in the grand review of the troops in Washington that followed the South's capitulation. Puffer himself often told people that he was present at Ford's Theatre on the night that President Lincoln was assassinated. After the war, he went to work for Alonzo Valentine in his knitting mill, and around 1880, he helped organize the Bennington Knitting Company, a leading manufacturer of ladies' and children's underwear. Later, he was connected with the Bennington Wax Paper Company and became a director of the Bennington County National Bank.

The oldest enlistee from Bennington appears to be Luke Walton, who signed up at the age of fifty-one. He is buried in the Village Cemetery and will be mentioned later, but his age calls attention to the range of age of volunteers.

Charles Cole's Grave

Sergeant Charles G. Cole (1829–1896) was also from Bennington and enlisted in August 1861 at the age of thirty-two. He entered the service as a corporal in Company A of the Fourth Vermont Regiment and was wounded at the Battle of Fredericksburg on December 13, 1862. Shortly after the battle, Cole was promoted to sergeant but was discharged, due to his wounds, a few months later. Once he returned to Bennington, he went into business and had an interest in the Eagle Square Company. He also ran a clothing store on Main Street in the old Opera House. In addition to men's clothing, he carried tea, coffee, guns and sporting goods. He died in 1896 at his home at 82 North Street.

Olin Scott's Grave

Olin Scott (1832–1913), who became one of Bennington's most prominent industrialists, was born in 1832 in a house that once stood just north of today's Veterans' Home. Except for a few years as a clerk in the Troy/Albany area, he spent his whole life in Bennington. At the beginning of the war, he helped raise volunteers for the army and drilled with them before they went off to the front, but he was needed in his mill for the war effort and did not go into battle. Not being able to go, he hired a man to take his place, without procuring an exemption for himself, it should be noted. At that time, Scott was the only mechanical engineer in the United States who was experienced in the construction of gunpowder mills, so he was much more valuable to the military as a civilian.

Grave of Colonel Olin Scott. *Author's collection.*

Although he never served in the Civil War, he later joined the Vermont State Guard and was made colonel, hence the rank of Colonel Scott on his tombstone. After the war, Olin Scott lived on Pleasant Street in a house that still stands near the factory he built. Scott is of special interest to students of the Civil War because he was the founder of the Bennington Machine Works, the company that produced virtually all the machinery used in the manufacture of gunpowder during the war. At one time, the business was valued at $2 million. In fact, his Olin Scott Fund still gives more than $1 million annually for scholarships to Vermont students from offices at 407 Main Street.

Frank Ray's Grave

Frank Ray (1837–1864), a Bennington native, was appointed sergeant in Company G of the First Vermont Cavalry in 1861. He was commissioned first lieutenant the following year and promoted to captain in 1863. The following year, he was wounded at Yellow Tavern before seeing action at Fisher's Hill in September 1864. Although his epitaph says that he died at

Grave of Captain Frank Ray. *Author's collection.*

Fisher's Hill, he was actually killed in the Battle of Tom's Brook on October 9, 1864, in the Union victory that gave control of the Shenandoah Valley to the Army of the Potomac. His tombstone is an especially handsome one and shows a sword resting atop a flag that is draped over the marker.

Newton Stone's Grave

Grave of Lieutenant Newton Stone. *Author's collection.*

Lieutenant Newton Stone (1836–1864), was born in Readsboro, the son of a minister. In May 1861, at the age of twenty-three and shortly after he had been admitted to the bar, he joined the army. He volunteered to fight with Company A of the Second Vermont Infantry, formed by Bennington-area men. Stone was promoted several times, first to captain, then to major and, finally, to colonel. On the second day of the Battle of the Wilderness in May 1864, Stone was on the front lines when a bullet hit him in the fleshy part of the leg. He was taken back to an aid station, where the wound was quickly dressed. Stone hobbled to his horse and rode back into the thick of the fighting, where his men greeted him with a rousing cheer. It was then that a bullet hit him in the head, killing him instantly. He was twenty-six at the time of his death. His body was brought back to Bennington for burial with honors along with this message from his commander, General Lewis Grant: "He was beloved by his command, and by all who knew him, a good officer, gallant by nature, prompt in his duties and urbane in his manner."[99] From his regiment of nearly 2,000 men and officers, no fewer than 751 were killed or wounded during the course of the war.

Edward and Henry Selden's Graves

Edward Selden (1824–1862) entered the navy in 1841 as a midshipman, and by the beginning of the war, he had advanced to the level of lieutenant. Then, in 1862, he decided to transfer to the army and fought with the

Second Vermont Infantry as a private. Within a few months of his transfer, he contracted a disease and died at Harrison's Landing, Virginia, on August 4, 1862.

The same monument also commemorates Edward's older brother, Henry Selden (1821–1865). Henry was appointed to West Point in 1839 and graduated with the class of 1843. He had been a classmate of Ulysses S. Grant. After graduation, Henry became a career officer with the army and moved up in the ranks from first lieutenant to colonel. He served with the U.S. Infantry in the Third Seminole War, and at the time of his death in 1865, he was commanding a volunteer regiment on the western frontier of New Mexico. He had been posted there to deal with border and Indian problems during the war. The now-abandoned Fort Selden near Las Cruces, New Mexico, was named in his honor.

George Hicks's Grave

Grave of Captain George Hicks. *Author's collection.*

George Hicks (1840–1864) volunteered for the army at the age of twenty-one. He was raised in Bennington and enrolled as a student at Williams College in 1862, but he left the school to enlist as a corporal in Company A of the Fourteenth Vermont Infantry. He fought at the Battle of Gettysburg and was promoted to sergeant, then commissioned a first lieutenant in Company F of the Seventeenth Vermont Infantry. Hicks was brevetted captain for gallantry and meritorious service in the charge near Shand's House, Virginia. At Petersburg, in 1864, the coal miners from Pennsylvania dug a long mine shaft underneath the Confederate defenses and set off an enormous explosion to make a hole in the defensive lines. The hole created was much more than a breech. The blast made a huge caldron in the earth, the size of a football field and nearly as deep. George Hicks was part of the detachment that was sent into "the Crater" immediately after the explosion. Although the blast did make a hole in the Rebel line as predicted, it was so deep that the soldiers who ran into the crater couldn't get up the steep sides, and the Confederates shot hundreds of them, "like shooting fish in a barrel." Captain Hicks was one of those killed in the slaughter. His body was recovered and brought home to Bennington for burial.

Lyman F. Abbott's Grave

Lyman Frederick Abbott (1839–1920), the youngest of eight children, was born in Massachusetts and lived there until his family moved to Bennington around 1855. His sister was married to Henry Bradford, the founder of the H.E. Bradford and Company Mills on upper Main Street, and the young Lyman went to work for his brother-in-law. Bradford made woolen cloth and cotton knit goods throughout the Civil War period. When the war began, many men in Vermont volunteered, but by 1863, the steady stream of volunteers had dried up and a draft had to be imposed. At the time, the rule was that if you were drafted you had several options. You could serve in the army or pay a $300 fee or find your own substitute directly. Many men of means hired replacements, and that's what Lyman did. Abbott paid the commutation fee and continued his work at the mill for the duration of the war. In 1873, when Henry Bradford died, Lyman Abbott took over the business and became senior partner. For the rest of his life, he was a respected member of the business community and active in the town. In 1880, he ran as a Republican for representative in the state legislature and won. He became a member of the Bennington Historical Society and the Bennington Battle Monument Association, as well as a director of the First National Bank of Bennington.

Thomas Austin Hutchins's Grave

In 1861, musicians from Bennington and Whitingham formed a military band, which Thomas Austin Hutchins (1833–1909) joined. The band was attached to the Second Vermont Regiment but was discharged at the end of the year for budgetary reasons. While some reenlisted with other units, Hutchins and some others did not. Before the war, Hutchins had worked for Lyons and Thatcher in their famous United States Pottery in Bennington. Later, he went into the grocery business in the Cutler Block on Main Street, and still later, he became connected with the Glastenbury Electric Railroad. He died in 1909, and this marker was placed here, clearly showing how proud he was to have been a member of the regimental band.

Governor Hiland Hall's Grave

Hiland Hall (1795–1885), who went on to become one of Bennington's most prominent men, was born in 1795. After studying the law, Hall was admitted to the bar in 1819 and served many public offices during his lifetime. He was elected as a congressman and then governor from 1858 to 1860. He is discussed at greater length throughout this book.

Colonel George Harrington's Grave

George Dana Harrington (1823–1879) accepted a commission as captain on May 3, 1862, and was twice brevetted, first as major and then as lieutenant colonel in the U.S. Volunteers for his meritorious services during the war. He was stationed for most of the time at Camp Chase in Columbus, Ohio, and discharged in the fall of 1865. He died in 1879 after moving to Washington, D.C., but his body was returned to Bennington for burial.

CATHOLIC CEMETERY ON MAIN STREET, BEHIND THE BENNINGTON MUSEUM

Although often overlooked, this cemetery, just to the west of the Bennington Museum, contains the graves of nearly twenty Civil War soldiers, including Private Edward Grace's.

Private Edward Grace's Grave

Edward Grace (1832–1864) enlisted at the beginning of the war as a private in Company A of the Second Vermont Regiment. He was born in Ireland but came to this country to escape the Irish famine. He then joined the army at the age of twenty-seven and marched off with Captain James Walbridge and the rest of the "Bennington Union Guard," as they were called then. On May 5, 1864, in the terrible Battle of the Wilderness, he was killed in action fighting for his new country.

Bennington

Civil War Memorial

Located in front of the Bennington Museum at 75 Main Street

The bronze marker mounted on the large boulder in front of the Grandma Moses Schoolhouse is the most important monument to Civil War soldiers in Bennington. One would expect to see a tablet with a long list of soldiers' names commemorating their service, but this one is more subtle. The memorial was commissioned in 1929 by a committee headed by museum director John Spargo, members of the Bennington Historical Society and the American Legion. They commissioned the young California-born sculptor William Gordon Huff (1903–1993) to design it. This was to be Huff's first major commission. While working on the sculpture, he lived in Bennington, and it is said that some of the models used for his portraits were Bennington men. When the relief was completed, Huff returned to California, and most of his future work was done out there. As a result, his work is little known in the East.[100]

Depicted are four officers on horseback reviewing their troops as they march off to war. They are identified from foreground to background as:

1. General George Stannard (1820–1886). One of the most important of Vermont's commanders, Stannard was born in the Vermont town named Georgia and grew up in St. Albans. In June 1861, he was elected lieutenant colonel of the Second Vermont Regiment and was later made brigadier general and brevet major general.

Civil War Memorial, Bennington. *Author's collection.*

2. BRIGADIER GENERAL EDWARD HASTINGS RIPLEY (1839–1915) of Rutland. He left Union College in Schenectady, New York, to enlist as a private but rose steadily to the rank of brigadier general by 1864. Ripley was given the honor of leading the Union troops into Richmond at the close of the war.

3. COLONEL WHEELOCK GRAVES VEAZEY (1835–1898) was born in Brentwood, New Hampshire, but spent most of his adult life in Rutland. He was selected to be included on the monument because he was the only Vermont man to be elected commander of the Grand Army of the Republic (GAR), a fraternal group of Civil War veterans. Veazey won the Medal of Honor at Gettysburg and then returned to Vermont to practice law, eventually becoming a judge on the bench of the Vermont Supreme Court.

4. COLONEL JAMES WALBRIDGE of Bennington led Bennington's Company A of the Second Regiment and will be discussed in much greater detail later.

One of the more interesting things about this relief is that it contains a nearly secret list of all the men who served from the town of Bennington. Surrounding the picture are olive leaves, and if you look closely, you'll see that each leaf bears the name of a Bennington veteran, some 337 names in total. By the time the memorial was unveiled on August 16, 1930, only a few of the men thus honored were still alive. The last Civil War veteran living in Bennington is reported to have been Moses J. Knapp, who died in 1934 at the age of ninety-four.

ABRAHAM LINCOLN STATUE

Located in front of the Bennington Museum at 75 Main Street

Statue of Abraham Lincoln by Clyde du Vernet Hunt. *Author's collection.*

It would be impossible to do a Civil War tour without mentioning the giant statue of Abraham Lincoln that stands in front of the museum. The statue was created in 1939 by native Vermonter Clyde du Vernet Hunt. Hunt's father served in the Civil War as a colonel in the Adjutant General's Department in Washington, D.C. The artist himself was born in 1861, the opening year of the war, and graduated from MIT. He received early encouragement from his famous uncles, painter William Morris Hunt and architect Richard Morris Hunt, who were both from Brattleboro. After studying art in Paris and setting up a studio there, Clyde returned to his home in Weathersfield Bow, Vermont, and split his time between there and Paris for the rest of his life. He died in 1941 at the age of eighty, two years after he put together this sculpture.

I say put together because that's really what he did. They were actually three different statues that had nothing to do with one another until Hunt combined them into this large composition. The figure of the boy was originally a stand-alone work called *Fils de France* and symbolized the rebirth of France after World War I. The sculpture of the woman was originally called *Nirvana* and was created to personify the quality of tranquility. Abraham Lincoln was always Lincoln, but he was originally meant to stand alone, too. When Hunt assembled these as a group, he called it simply *Lincoln*, but he said that it was meant to be a representation of Faith, Hope and Charity. The completed work was first displayed in front of the Illinois State Pavilion at the New York World's Fair in 1939. After Hunt's death, his heirs donated the group to the Bennington Museum. It was at that time that the museum's director, John Spargo, decided to rename it the *American Spirit*.

BENNINGTON MUSEUM AT 75 MAIN STREET

The Bennington Museum was founded as the Bennington Historical Association in 1852, so it will come as no surprise to learn that the museum has a large collection of Civil War artifacts.

U.S. Flag

The museum collection contains the flag that was made by the women of Bennington at the very beginning of the Civil War. They presented it to the volunteers of Company A, Second Vermont Regiment, in May 1861, when the men were mustered in at the Old First Church. On the stripes, they embroidered the words: "Presented to the Bennington Boys of '61 by the Ladies." The flag remained in Bennington and was not carried into battle. It was used ceremonially and was draped over the coffins of many veterans in the following years. The last surviving members of Company A donated it to the museum.

Flag made for "the Bennington Boys." *Bennington Museum, Bennington, Vermont.*

Key to Richmond's Libby Prison. *Bennington Museum, Bennington, Vermont.*

General Ripley Collection

In 1865, when the Confederates set fire to Richmond and abandoned the city, Brigadier General Edward Hastings Ripley of Rutland led the Northern troops into the city. Following his death, his family gave Ripley's papers and memorabilia to the museum. One important item is the key to Libby Prison, which he and his men liberated. Libby was considered second only to Andersonville when it came to brutal prisons, and many of the ten thousand men incarcerated there during the war died of starvation and disease. The notorious prison building itself survived the war and was moved to Chicago in 1889 to serve as a Civil War museum.

Cannon

Inside the battle of Bennington room, one of the brass field cannons captured from the British army during the Battle of Bennington is on display. This is the same field piece that was in front of the capital building in Montpelier in April 1861. It was fired at that time to mark the beginning of the special session of the general assembly called by Governor Erastus Fairbanks in response to Lincoln's request to send one regiment of Vermont soldiers to defend Washington, D.C. The assembly voted to send seven regiments.

Uniforms

The museum owns a large collection of Civil War uniforms, ceremonial swords and other military objects, which are occasionally exhibited.

Uniform worn by George Stannard while still a colonel in 1863. *Bennington Museum, Bennington, Vermont.*

Photographs

The museum collection includes hundreds of pictures of Bennington Civil War soldiers and related documents, most donated by their families in the years after the war. Many of the illustrations included in this book were found in their files.

MAJOR ALONZO VALENTINE'S HOUSE

300 Pleasant Street

On the north side of Pleasant Street, at the intersection with Valentine Street, is a large brick house painted white with red trim. It is hard to believe that directly behind this house stood one of the largest mill complexes in Bennington, the Valentine Knitting Company. The house itself was built

Home of Major Alonzo Valentine. *Author's collection.*

in 1863 by Luther Park for his daughter Alma L. Park Valentine and her husband, Major Alonzo B. Valentine (1830–1904), who was off fighting at the time. Alma's brother was Trenor Park, one of the wealthiest men in Vermont. He had made his fortune during the California gold rush and had just returned to build the Park McCullough House in North Bennington around the same time.

In 1824, Joel Valentine (1791–1866), Alonzo's father, purchased a woolen mill very near this spot. In 1845, he tore it down to build a more substantial three-story brick factory on the same site. At one point, the Valentine mills consisted of nearly a dozen buildings and employed more than 150 workers making cotton and wool shirts and drawers. When Norman Puffer, Vermont's youngest drummer boy, came home from the war, he worked in these mills before going on to make his own fortune. Major Valentine was discharged in 1865 and took over the operation of the mills following his father's death a year later. He oversaw the mill's expansion and made it into one of the most efficient and best-equipped mills in town. In 1884, the Valentine mills were destroyed by fire. Nearby is Valentine Street, named in his honor.

OLIN SCOTT'S HOUSE AND THE BENNINGTON MACHINE WORKS

324 Pleasant Street and 330 Pleasant Street

Olin Scott, who is buried in the Old Bennington Cemetery and discussed in more detail in that section, built this elaborate Italianate, stick-style house in 1887. It was next to the frame office and brick foundry buildings of his company, the Bennington Machine Works. Several of those buildings still survive today from the Civil War era. Scott began his business career in 1858, when he purchased the Bennington Iron Foundry on North Street. By 1865, he had taken over the Eagle Iron Foundry and Machine Shop and began to erect these buildings on Pleasant Street. When they were finished, he consolidated his business in this location and sold off the other mills. Scott made the machinery that was used to manufacture gunpowder during the Civil War. This was no small business, and in fact reports indicate that Olin Scott's company made the equipment for every powder mill in America, except one. In addition to gunpowder machinery, the Bennington Machine Works also manufactured equipment used to make paper and cut marble.

Home of Olin Scott. *Author's collection.*

BENNINGTON VILLAGE CEMETERY ON MORGAN STREET SOUTH OF MAIN STREET

There are more graves of Civil War veterans here than in any other cemetery in town, except the Veterans' Home. Nearly 120 have been interred here over the years.

Major Alonzo Valentine's Grave

Alonzo B. Valentine (1830–1904), born and raised in Bennington, caught "gold fever" in 1852 and went to California to work in the mines. He then spent two more years in the lumber business in Wisconsin before returning to Vermont. When he was commissioned lieutenant and entered the army as the quartermaster of the Tenth Vermont Regiment, he was thirty-two. He was promoted to captain and then brevet major in 1864 for meritorious service. He served for the duration of the war and was mustered out on June 28, 1865. Valentine fought in the Battles of the Wilderness, Spotsylvania,

Cold Harbor, Fisher's Hill and Petersburg. Following the war, he returned to Bennington, where he took over his father's mills when the elder Valentine died in 1866 and converted the woolen mill into a successful cotton-knitting mill. In fact, for a while, his mills were the largest in the state. As a community leader, he was instrumental in establishing Bennington's graded schools, and more than any other man, Valentine was responsible for the Vermont Soldiers' Home being in Bennington. He died in 1904 at the age of seventy-four.

Private Luke Walton's Grave

Earlier we listed Norman Puffer as Bennington's youngest soldier and noted that Luke Walton (1812–1896) was the oldest to enlist. Luke joined from Woodford in the winter

Top: Grave of Major Alonzo Valentine. *Author's collection.*

Bottom: Major Alonzo Valentine, photograph by Calvin Dart. *Bennington Museum, Bennington, Vermont.*

of 1863, when he was fifty-one years old. He served as a private in Company G of the First Vermont Cavalry and, in 1865, transferred to Company E. Walton lived until 1896 and is buried in this cemetery.

Major John Pratt's Grave

John Edward Pratt (1835–1882) was born in Bennington and entered the army in 1861 as a captain in Company A of the Fourth Vermont Regiment. He had recruited a group of men from Bennington to be Zouaves, but they were not accepted as such and entered as regular soldiers. At the Battle of the Wilderness in May 1864, Colonel George Foster, who was leading the Fourth Vermont Regiment, was shot in the leg and gave up his command to Major Pratt. The following month, Major Pratt was taken prisoner with his men at Weldon Railroad and paroled in March 1865. After he returned home, he built a fine house with a semicircular driveway on the south side of Union Street, halfway between South and Silver Streets, but it is no longer standing.

Grave of Major John Pratt. *Author's collection.*

Sergeant Alonzo Bigelow

Alonzo Bigelow (1827–1869) entered the service from Bennington in the early days of the war at the age of thirty-three. When his enlistment was up in 1864, he reenlisted and rose in rank from private to sergeant before the war's end. He was wounded in the chest at Funkstown and then wounded again at Spotsylvania before being taken as a prisoner of war at Fredericksburg. Just after the war, Alonzo married Mary Aldrich and worked as a cooper for most of his short life, dying in 1869 at the age of forty-two.

Captain William Cady

One of Bennington's most respected officers was Captain William H. Cady (1836–1879). In May 1861, he volunteered with the first group of soldiers for duty in Company A of the Second Vermont Regiment, known as the Bennington Union Guards. Initially, Frank E. Smith was elected lieutenant of the company, but Smith realized that he could not perform in that capacity. Instead, he entered in the ranks of the enlisted men as a private, at which time Cady took his commission as lieutenant. Sadly Smith was to die in the Battle of Fredericksburg, along with so many other Vermont men. Cady commanded his men bravely in the First Battle of Bull Run and every engagement thereafter. He was wounded in the hand at the Wilderness but otherwise escaped serious injury throughout the course of his service. When he was mustered out in 1864, he accepted a post in the new state militia as lieutenant colonel of the Eleventh Regiment. Throughout his life, William Cady was a popular man whom everybody liked. This aided him after the war when he ran various businesses in town, including the Stark House, one

Grave of Captain William Cady. *Author's collection.*

of the town's best hotels. He died suddenly in 1879, and his many mourners came to decorate his grave with an evergreen wreath, roses and laurel.

Private Henry Camp's Grave

Henry G. Camp (1846–1924) entered the army at the age of fourteen, making him one of the youngest soldiers from Bennington. He fought with Company A of the Fourth Vermont Infantry and was discharged due to wounds at the end of 1862. He reenlisted, however, in 1863, before his injuries had completely healed, and was taken as a prisoner of war at Weldon Railroad. By some miracle, he survived the notorious Andersonville prison camp. He weighed 179 pounds when he went into the prison and 77 pounds when he was freed. At the end of the war, he was mustered out but remained in army hospitals for several months before Joseph H. Loring went to Annapolis and brought the young soldier home. His Civil War experiences were remarkable. In addition to being wounded twice, he was incarcerated in at least thirteen different Confederate prisons and escaped once, only to be recaptured before he found the Union lines. His father and three brothers also enlisted in Vermont regiments. His father and one brother were killed, and another brother lost his arm. Private Camp recovered his health and remained in the area until his own death at the Soldiers' Home in 1924.

Private John Carpenter's Grave

John Draper Carpenter (1845–1916) entered the army as a substitute for Laurer F. Fowler of Jamaica, Vermont, in September 1863 after Lincoln's first draft of 300,000 men. He became a private in Company K of the Third Vermont Regiment and then transferred to Company E of the Eleventh Vermont Regiment. Carpenter was wounded at the Battle of Cedar Creek but recovered and served through the end of the war. He was a longtime resident of Vermont and was married twice, having twenty children before his death at the Soldiers' Home in Bennington following a short illness.

Private Orrick Cressa's Grave

When Orrick Cressa (1819–1898) died, the newspaper called him the "Bennington Hermit" because he had been living an isolated life in the hills for many years. In 1862, at the age of thirty-seven, he enlisted as a private in the army and served for nine months with Company E of the Tenth Vermont Regiment. His obituary noted that every time he received his quarterly pension money from the army, he would spend it on a large supply of tobacco. He lived primarily off seasonal jobs such as cutting firewood and logging.

Quartermaster Henry Cushman's Grave

Henry Theodore Cushman, the founder of H.T. Cushman Company, was buried in this cemetery in 1922. He served as the quartermaster for the Fourth Vermont Regiment from 1862 until 1864. Later, he became a prominent member of the community, and his life is described in much greater detail later in this book.

Corporal John Evans's Grave

Born in Woodford, John H. Evans (1839–1916) died of pneumonia at his home on Main Street in Bennington in 1916. Evans had served in Company

Grave of Henry T. Cushman. *Author's collection.*

A of the Fourth Vermont Regiment from 1861 until 1863 but was stricken with typhoid near Harrison's Landing. While in the hospital in Philadelphia, he fell in love with his nurse, Miss Mary Sewell, and married her at the close of the war. They lived in Philadelphia until her death twenty years later, and then he moved back to Bennington, where he entered the lumber business. He remained in town until his own death.

Sergeant Frederick Godfrey's Grave

Frederick Godfrey (1841–1923) was born in Bennington and enlisted in Company A of the Fourth Vermont Regiment in August 1861. He reenlisted once and served through the end of the war. Although he was injured three times, each wound proved to be minor. He was demoted on one occasion and served with the troops that marched into New York City to put down the Draft Riots in 1863. After being mustered out, he served on the Bennington police force for forty-four years and was elected county sheriff.

Private George Harwood's Grave

George Hibbard Harwood (1845–1925) was born in North Bennington in 1845. He enlisted with Company A of the Fourteenth Vermont Regiment at the age of eighteen as drummer boy and went with the other nine-months men from Bennington to serve under Captain "Ranse" Gore. After he returned to Bennington, he worked in various mills and became an active member of the local volunteer fire department in which he served for fifty years.

Corporal Edward Payson Hathaway's Grave

Edward Payson Hathaway (1841–1933) was born in Bennington and enlisted with Captain Gore's men as a corporal in Company A of the Fourteenth Vermont Regiment. At the time of his death, he was one of the last surviving members of his company. He passed away at his home on Gage Street in 1933. During his nine-month tour of duty, Hathaway's unit defended Washington, D.C., and then took part in the Battle of Gettysburg. Back home, he taught school for several years before becoming a farmer, passing away at the age of ninety-two.

Grave of Corporal Edward Hathaway. *Author's collection.*

Private George Marsh's Grave

In June 1861, George M. Marsh (1832–1893) joined the young men from Bennington who enlisted with the band. They spent the rest of that year leading the troops in processions and drills, but in December, they were mustered out by a special order of the War Department in an austerity effort. Marsh spent his life working in various mills around town and was working as a guard on the town poor farm when he passed away at the age of seventy-one.

William Murphy's Grave

William E. Murphy (1833–1904) enlisted in the army when the initial call came for troops in 1961. He was mustered in as a corporal of Company A, Second Vermont Regiment, and taken prisoner only a month later.

Following his parole, he returned to his regiment only to be wounded at the Battle of the Wilderness on May 5, 1864, and then was mustered out in June due to those injuries. He became a carpenter in Bennington and lived in a boardinghouse at 112 East Main Street.

Sergeant Samuel Norton's Grave

Samuel B. Norton (1839–1864) enlisted in the Thirteenth Vermont Regiment as a corporal at the age of twenty-two. After enlisting again in 1864, he was promoted to sergeant of Company F in the Seventeenth Vermont Regiment, which was made up mostly of men from Bennington and Windham County. Norton was killed in action while charging the Confederate breastworks at Petersburg that June. The newspaper reported that he had been shot in the head and died instantly. His commanding officer, Lieutenant Hicks, reported that he was highly esteemed by his fellow soldiers and was "prompt and ready to do his duty at all times and in all places." His comrades buried him under a peach tree in a garden near where he fell. Later, his body was retrieved and a funeral service was held for him in Bennington's Episcopal Church that August.

BRADFORD MILLS

751 Main Street

In the 1850s, Henry E. Bradford established the company that became one of the pioneer firms manufacturing wool and cotton knit goods in Bennington, H.E. Bradford and Company. Over the following decades, he enlarged his mill several times and built a beautiful house right across the street. When the original mill burned in 1865, he erected a new factory, which is the one still standing on East Main Street today. His mills, along with others in town, had to shut down from time to time during the Civil War due to a shortage of raw materials, but when they had the cotton, they worked at peak capacity. This was the company in which Lyman Abbott, Henry Bradford's brother-in-law, became a partner in 1863. Abbott has been mentioned earlier as one of the men who hired a substitute to serve in the army in his place.

BENNINGTON POWDER COMPANY ON EAST MAIN STREET

The Bennington Powder Company was established by William Russell, Isaac Weeks and James B. Morgan in 1858 to manufacture gunpowder. During the Civil War, it was one of the smaller companies of about twenty that received government contracts for gunpowder nationwide. The mill, then located near the East Main Street entrance to today's Bennington Bypass, averaged nearly a ton of gunpowder per day during the course of the war. It is interesting to note that although one would guess that the Civil War was good for the gunpowder business, it actually was not. Olin Scott, the man who produced the machinery used to make gunpowder, stated that more explosives were used in times of peace than in times of war. He argued the point by saying that more powder was used to dig the Hoosac Railroad Tunnel than was consumed by the Union army during the entire war effort.

There were two explosions at these gunpowder mills during the war, one on October 15, 1861, and a second on January 29, 1864, but luckily no one was killed in those. Shortly after the war, on August 27, 1867, the Bennington Powder Company exploded once again. This time, however, three men were killed. The newspapers reported that the blast could be heard from North Adams to Troy. That explosion occurred when a workman hit a nail with a hammer causing a spark. The mill was rebuilt, but in 1869, its machinery was dismantled. The Bennington site was converted into a wood pulp mill.

RANSOM O. GORE'S FARM

Beech Street turns into Gore Road as it goes up the hill east of town. At the top of the rise is the location of the eighty-acre farm owned by Captain Ransom O. Gore, and although his house burned down long ago, his pastures are still there. When Gore was twenty-eight, he helped form Company A of the Fourteenth Vermont Regiment. After the Battle of Gettysburg, Captain Gore was discharged and returned home. He rejected an offer to command another unit after several members of his family came down with typhoid fever. He was needed at home to take care of the family, and he remained on the farm for the rest of his eighty-seven years.

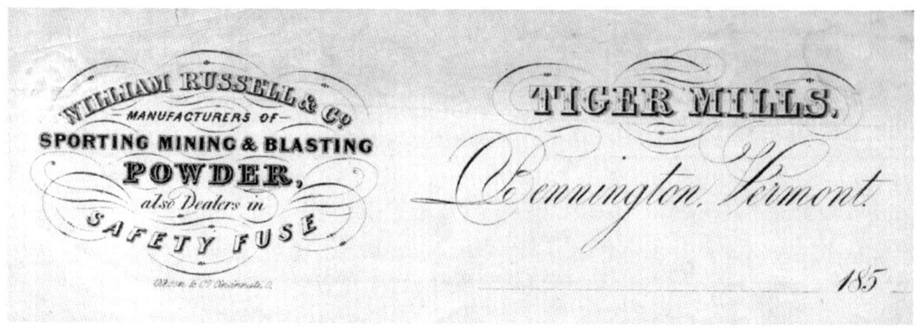

Letterhead for William Russell's gunpowder mills. *Bennington Museum, Bennington, Vermont.*

BENNINGTON FREE LIBRARY ON THE CORNER OF EAST MAIN AND SILVER STREETS

The brick building that stands on the corner of Main and Silver Streets was the town's first public library. It was originally built and donated to the town in 1865 by Trenor Park and Seth B. Hunt. When the library was opened, it had shops that were rented out on the first floor facing Main Street and a large auditorium on the top floor that was used for lectures and public gatherings. The first important event hosted by the library was the memorial service held immediately following the assassination of President Lincoln.

PARK LAWN CEMETERY ON SOUTH STREET (ROUTE 7)

Although a relatively new cemetery by Bennington standards, Park Lawn still has the graves of around twenty-five Civil War veterans.

Captain Ransom Gore's Grave

In 1862, Ransom O. Gore (1834–1920) accepted a captain's commission with Company A of the Fourteenth Vermont Infantry. His unit was composed of Bennington men who volunteered to serve for a period of nine months. The officers of the Fourteenth met in Rutland on September 24, 1862, and elected William T. Nichols of Rutland as their colonel.

Nathaniel R. Hall, a son of Hiland Hall, was elected major and Ransom Gore captain. When Company A took part in the Battle of Gettysburg, it was lucky because not one of the 101 men in the company was killed. Many were wounded, including Captain Gore—who was hit three times by shrapnel—but no one died of his wounds. Captain Gore was discharged after his term expired and returned to his Bennington farm.

Grave of Captain Ransom Gore. *Author's collection.*

Martin Biggs's Grave

Although born in Louisville, Kentucky, Martin I. Biggs (1846–1916) enlisted with the Ninety-third New York Regiment. When he was mustered out, he settled in Troy but later moved to Bennington to be near his son, who lived on Division Street. Martin remained there for nearly twenty-five years. During the last few months of his life, he moved to the Soldiers' Home, where he died in 1916.

Senator Irving Gibson's Grave

Irving Edson Gibson (1846–1927) was born in Florence, New York, and enlisted with the army at the very end of 1863. He served as a private in Company A of the Fourth Vermont Regiment and was wounded at the Battle of the Wilderness in May 1864, although he recovered and served through the end of the war. Later, Gibson owned a general store at 67 East Main Street, became president of the Bennington County National Bank and bought the Bennington Gas Company for a reported $20,000. He served as a state senator from 1894 to 1896 and lived to be eighty-one.

Private Cornelius Lambert's Grave

At the age of nineteen, native of Cambridge, New York Cornelius M. Lambert (1843–1919) enlisted as a private in Company E of the Fifth Vermont Regiment. He was discharged with a disability on February 16, 1862, but eventually regained his health. Lambert returned to Bennington and spent the rest of his life manufacturing and selling grave monuments. Most of that time, he was in the employ of A.I. Loomis & Company and lived at 17 Gage Street.

VERMONT SOLDIERS' HOME

325 North Street

The large white clapboard house that now serves as the administrative offices for the Vermont Soldiers' Home was originally built in 1860 as the summer home of the wealthy businessman Seth B. Hunt. Hunt called the property Maple Grove after the sugar maples that once covered his property. He was born in Bennington but moved to New York, where he made his fortune. The house originally had eleven rooms, and traces of the old interior are still visible today. In front of the house, near the modern gazebo, Hunt constructed a 100-foot round basin for a giant fountain that shot water 196 feet into the air. It was fed by water from a reservoir several miles to the east. The water had a fall of 300 feet and was piped into the fountain at great pressure through an eight-inch pipe. Many guidebooks of the period touted it as the highest natural fountain in the world. The house itself cost $60,000 to build, but the fountain cost $20,000; so it was obviously a very important part of the property and a source of great pride for both Hunt and the town. The fountain was turned off in 1962 due to drought and was never restored.[101]

Seth Hunt was generous to his hometown and partnered with Trenor Park to build the town's public library in 1865. In 1880, when Hunt died, Trenor Park bought the house and property from Hunt's heirs with the idea of establishing the "Trenor W. Park Home for Destitute Children and Women." That idea ended abruptly two years later in 1882, when Trenor Park died suddenly on a trip to Panama. At the time, the State of Vermont was looking for a place to build a home for old and sick Civil War veterans. At Alonzo Valentine's urging, the state acquired this property, and in 1886,

Vermont Soldiers' Home. *Author's collection.*

the Soldiers' Home of Vermont was chartered. It took over the property, which included the house, a farm and two hundred acres of land. At first, it was able to accommodate twenty veterans, but the house filled up quickly, and the following year, work began on a large addition that was to hold thirty-eight more residents. In 1891, a hospital and chapel were added, and the facility has continued to grow ever since.

In 1887, Colonel Robert John Coffey (1842–1901) was selected to be the first superintendent of the Soldiers' Home. Colonel Coffey was born in Canada, but by the time the Civil War began, he was a living in Montpelier and among the first to volunteer for three months' duty. He enlisted with Company F of the New England Guards and took part in the very first real battle of the war, called Big Bethel. When his initial term of duty expired, he reenlisted as a sergeant with Company F of the Second Vermont Infantry Regiment. With the Second Vermont, he fought in the Battles of Lee's Mills, several battles in front of Richmond under General McClellan, South Mountain, Antietam, Fredericksburg, Gettysburg and others. During the Battle at Banks Ford, Virginia, on May 4, 1863, Coffey single-handedly captured seven Confederates—two officers and five regulars—for which he was awarded the Medal of Honor. Eyewitness accounts said that the Confederate soldiers were shocked when they discovered that Coffey had been completely alone at the time of their capture. Later that same year, he was badly wounded and mustered out of the army as a result of those injuries.

When he returned home, he went into the hotel business upstate for a few years. Then in 1887, he became the unanimous choice for superintendent of the new Veterans' Home here. His wife was appointed to act as matron, which was a common practice in those days. Coffey worked in Bennington until his death in 1901 at the age of fifty-nine, at which time his body was returned to Montpelier for burial in his family's plot.

Captain George Davis was another Civil War Medal of Honor winner who lived at the home. He enlisted early as a three-month man with the First Vermont Regiment and then reenlisted, serving until the end of the war. Although wounded several times, Captain Davis was never slowed down. He won the Medal of Honor for his bravery in Maryland at the Battle of Monocacy on July 9, 1864. There, he and his men held the approaches to two bridges against assaults from a superior force of Confederates and thus delayed General Early's advance on Washington. Davis was from Burlington and, after he passed away at the Veterans' Home, was buried there.

VETERANS' CEMETERY

This cemetery is located immediately behind the Vermont Soldiers' Home. The graves are very easy to locate. The first row behind the cannon is row A, followed by row B, then C and so on. The graves are numbered beginning with number one along the driveway to the north. Many Civil War veterans, more than 160 men from all parts of the state, are buried here.

Civil War Cannon

At the base of the flagpole is a twelve-pounder Napoleon, model 1857, Civil War cannon. Most of the Bennington men who were part of artillery units would have been trained to fire this type of cannon because it was the most

Veterans' Cemetery. *Author's collection.*

common field piece used during the war. This gun has a range of 1,600 yards (just about a mile), so troops near the battle monument could be within range of the Veterans' Home cannon. It was a large operation, requiring seven men to fire it and teams of horses to pull the cannon and caissons filled with ammunition and equipment.

Sergeant John Connelly's Grave (A10)

John C. Connelly (1839–1899) was twenty-three when he entered the army in August 1862. Over the next three years, he had a very active military record. Originally, Connelly was mustered into Company C of the Fourteenth Vermont Infantry, but he was demoted and mustered out in July 1863. In January 1864, he enlisted again into Company G of the First Vermont Cavalry, and before long, he was promoted to first sergeant. Later that year, he was made quartermaster sergeant. Connelly was wounded in October 1864 and deserted in November, only to return the following spring.

At that time, he transferred to Company E before finally being mustered out in August 1865. In 1899, he died and was buried here at the home.

Private Henry Downs's Grave (B14)

Henry W. Downs (1844–1898) of Pownal was eighteen years old when he joined the army. In 1862, he enlisted in Company A of the Fourteenth Vermont Infantry Volunteers before being wounded at Gettysburg. After he was mustered out, he reenlisted with Company A of the Second Vermont Infantry. He was wounded once again at Petersburg and mustered out at war's end. Downs died in 1898.

Anson Aldrich's Grave (B16)

Anson L. Aldrich (1835–1898) was a direct descendant of George Aldrich, an early settler who came from England to the Massachusetts Bay Colony in 1631. Although Anson Aldrich was born in Massachusetts, he moved to Bennington in 1859 to marry Mary Luther. They were divorced at the end of the war, which was uncommon in those days. Anson's service record is interesting but not unique. He enlisted in August 1861 with Company A of the Fourth Vermont Infantry volunteers and deserted in September 1863 after the Battle of Gettysburg. A year later, he reenlisted in a New York regiment under the name of Anson B. Eldridge and served through the end of the war. Deserting and returning was not unusual during the Civil War, and soldiers often left to attend to chores like planting and harvesting crops.

Corporal Luther Eames's Grave (B20)

Luther Eames (1834–1905) was born and raised in Wilmington, Vermont. He enlisted in September 1861 as a private in Company I of the Fourth Vermont Infantry. During the war, the Fourth lost more men in proportion to its total than any other Vermont regiment. Eames reenlisted two years later, after having been promoted to corporal, and was transferred to Company F of the same regiment. In 1864, he was taken prisoner at the Battle of Weldon Railroad and paroled about a year later. Parole was a typical way for the armies to handle prisoners during the Civil War. Neither the North nor the South could afford to take care of the large numbers of prisoners captured in battle, so they made prisoner exchanges on a mass scale. Even when there were not enough troops to exchange, the Confederates would parole soldiers and return them to the North with the understanding that they would not reenlist again during the term of their parole. This method seems to have actually been effective. After Private Eames was paroled, he returned to Bennington County and lived to be seventy-one, passing away in 1905.

Corporal Edward Carroll's Grave (C 21)

Edward Carroll (1839–1906) was one of many soldiers who was born in Ireland and immigrated to this country with his family during the great famine. Irish and German immigrants made up a large part of the Northern forces during the war. New York, in fact, had an entire Irish Brigade, which was composed entirely of men from Ireland, some of whom were signed up the minute they stepped off the boat. Edward Carroll enlisted as a private in the army in Bennington in 1861. At first, he served with Company G of the First Vermont Cavalry, but he was taken prisoner in March 1862. He was released in September of the same year and then reenlisted the following year before being taken prisoner again. After he was paroled, he was promoted to corporal and transferred to Company E, where he served until the end of the war.

Private John Slocum's Grave (D 12)

John Slocum (1818–1900) was a good example of someone who frequently deserted and returned. He entered the military as a private in 1861 at the old age of forty-three. In August 1862, he deserted but returned in October 1863. Then he reenlisted in December 1863 and deserted again in July 1864. Once more, he returned to his company in September 1864 and was finally mustered out at the end of the war in June 1865. It is speculation, but it would appear that he might have been a farmer and deserted each year so that he could take part in the harvest.

Private William Jones's Grave (E 13)

William R. Jones (1840–1895) was another soldier born in Ireland who enlisted at the beginning of the war and reenlisted so that he could serve through the final battles of 1865. Jones was wounded at the Battle of the Wilderness on May 5, 1864, like so many other Vermont men.

Joseph Carbo's Grave (E 18)

In 1865, Joseph Carbo (1833–1901) entered the service as a substitute at the age of thirty-two. He was one of the men who was not drafted but volunteered to replace someone else in order to earn the $450 bounty being offered at the time. He served with the Eighth Vermont Infantry for six months, until the end of the war.

Private Edwin Hall's Grave (F20)

Edwin Clifton Hall (1845–1913) fought with Company C of the Fifteenth Vermont Infantry and then Company G of the Tenth Vermont Infantry. In 1862, at the age of nineteen, he enlisted with the nine-month men, was mustered out and then reenlisted in 1863. He was wounded at Cold Harbor in 1864 and again in 1865 at Petersburg before finally being mustered out for the last time at the end of the war. He died at the Soldiers' Home in 1913 after living there for a few years.

CHARLES HICKS'S HOME

593 Rice Lane Near Matteson Road

In 1822, Charles Hicks purchased a large farm on Rice Lane from Daniel Marsh. Hicks was a stagecoach driver and, as such, was frequently on the road. This might be why he was able to easily move escaped slaves on their way to freedom in Canada through this part of the state. One of the few documents giving proof that the Underground Railroad was active in Bennington is a letter that tells of the day in 1843 when Hicks helped a black man escaping with his wife and three children. He gave them a place to stay overnight and then sent his son, Henry, with them to guide them to the next safe house in Shaftsbury. The house he lived in has been modernized, but it is still here to remind us of Hicks's dedication to the cause of the abolition of slavery.

Major James Walbridge's birthplace

North Bennington Road at the Corner of Murphy Road

In 1826, James Walbridge, whose life will be described in greater detail later, was born in the red one-story house on the south side of the road just east of the Paper Mill covered bridge. The house was built by General Ebenezer Walbridge of Revolutionary War fame and, at one time, had a second story. In the twentieth century, a fire badly damaged the house, which caused the top floor to be removed and the roof lowered, but the first floor of the original house still survives.

Birthplace of Major James Walbridge. *Author's collection.*

Hinsdellville Cemetery on North Bennington Road (Route 67) at Wilkie Way

Even though small, the Hinsdellville Cemetery has the graves of at least twenty-five Civil War veterans.

Private Allen Canady's Grave

Allen S. Canady (1847–1889) was a private in Company E of the Tenth Vermont Regiment. He was born in Heath, Massachusetts, but lived most of his life in Bennington before moving to Wilmington, Vermont. He died there of consumption at the age of forty-three. Canady had been wounded at Cold Harbor and was discharged because of those wounds. The newspaper referred to him as a hardworking and industrious farmer who, at his death, had almost paid off the mortgage on the family farm.

Private Wales Puffer's Grave

Wales Puffer (1837–1880) was a musician who signed up with Bennington's band in June 1861, along with his younger brother Norman Puffer, who has been mentioned earlier. In December 1861, the War Department cut the budget for musicians, and most of the members of the Second Vermont Regiment band returned home, including Wales.

North Bennington

Henry T. Cushman's Home and Mill

Water Street

A familiar name in Bennington is that of Henry Theodore Cushman (1844–1922), the founder of H.T. Cushman Company. His large furniture manufacturing company operated in these stone mills well into the twentieth century. Cushman was born in Bennington, and when he was quite young, his father died; so the boy had to take over the family's clothing store on Main Street. Henry was just seventeen, technically underage, when he enlisted in 1862. Because of his business experience, he was appointed quartermaster of the Fourth Vermont Infantry Volunteers. Even though he was probably the youngest quartermaster in the army, he saw considerable service in the field as a staff officer, and his superiors noted that he was "not only an excellent quartermaster, but a brave and gallant soldier." At the Battle of the Wilderness, he was singled out for his bravery. At one point during the war, he was in charge of a small detail of about thirty men when they ran into the famous Confederate guerrilla Colonel John Singleton Mosby. They skirmished with Mosby briefly before they managed to get away, but after the war, Cushman and Mosby struck up a friendly correspondence that lasted for several years.

At the war's end, Cushman returned to Bennington and, in 1867, married Hiland Hall's granddaughter. In fact, they were married in the stone house across the street from the mill and lived there from 1867 until 1922. Their house then was converted into the furniture showroom for the Cushman

Home of Henry Cushman. *Author's collection.*

factory. When Henry first came home, he began to make small stationery novelties like erasers for the ends of pencils in a mill that stood where the North Bennington library is today. Eventually, he expanded into the furniture business, for which his company is best known.[102]

HILAND HALL'S HOME

Park Street

At the beginning of the Civil War, ex-Governor Hiland Hall was living in the family farmhouse next to what is now the Park McCullough Mansion. In 1858, Hall was elected governor of Vermont and reelected the following year, serving two one-year terms. He was always an outspoken critic of slavery, and in his first speech as governor, he denounced that "peculiar institution." In 1861, he led the Vermont delegation at a "Peace Congress" aimed at avoiding the war, but it failed in its mission. During his later years, Governor Hall spent much of his time indulging in his passion for historical research.

Home of Governor Hiland Hall. *Author's collection.*

FIRST NATIONAL BANK OF NORTH BENNINGTON

Corner of Bank and Main Streets

In 1863, as a way to finance the Civil War, Congress established a national banking system. It required anyone wishing to form a national bank to have one-third of their capital invested in U.S. government securities, and that helped raise the money that the country desperately needed. Trenor Park and Hiland Hall gathered a group of influential townspeople together on January 5, 1864, invested $400,000 and laid the groundwork for this bank, which opened that same year. The following year, another $100,000 in capital was added, making it the largest bank in the state at that time.

NORTH BENNINGTON RAILROAD STATION

Main and Depot Streets

Although the beautiful old train station was built after the Civil War, this was always the location of an important railroad depot and a connecting point for trains heading north to Rutland and beyond. Mrs. Abraham Lincoln rode on these tracks in August 1863 and again in early September 1864, when she and her son returned to Washington from a vacation at the Equinox House in Manchester. The whole family, including Abraham Lincoln, had made plans to return to Manchester the following year for their summer holiday, but Lincoln's assassination in April 1865 put an end to that dream.

Earlier, the body of John Brown had passed through this junction on its way to burial in 1859, following his execution. During the Civil War, troop trains and the shipment of weaponry made this a very active railroad line.

GRANDVIEW NORTH BENNINGTON CEMETERY ON GRANDVIEW STREET AT LAMB ROAD

Nearly twenty-five Civil War veterans are buried in the Grandview Cemetery, which is located just across the town line in Shaftsbury.

Private Samuel Rogers's Cenotaph

Although Samuel M. Rogers (1840–1862) is not buried here, there is a marker, called a cenotaph, erected by his family. This was more common at the time because it was difficult, expensive and sometimes logistically impossible to bring a body back from the front. Private Samuel Rogers is actually buried in the Fredericksburg National Cemetery in Virginia. In 1862, he was a member of Company I of the Third Vermont Infantry when he died of disease in a Fredericksburg hospital at the age of twenty-two.

Private John Minott's Grave

John H. Minott (1841–1862) is listed as being buried in this cemetery, and there is a marker for his parents; however, his own grave has not yet been identified. He was nineteen in 1861 when he signed up to fight with Company A of the Fourth Vermont Infantry Volunteers. He saw action at Lee's Mill and Antietam and was killed during the Battle of Fredericksburg in 1862. He had just turned twenty-one.

Oliver D. Green's Grave

In 1862, Private Oliver Green (1829–1891) enlisted in Company G of the First Vermont Cavalry and became a prisoner of war at the Battle of Brandy Station. He was sent to one of the most notorious prisons in the South, Andersonville, where he remained for nearly a year before being paroled. Conditions at Andersonville were so bad that life expectancy was measured in weeks, not years. Nearly thirteen thousand soldiers died there of disease and malnutrition. After the war, the commander of the prison, Captain Henry Wirz, was tried and executed for war crimes. Green was one of the lucky ones who survived. He died in 1891.

Colonel James Hicks Walbridge's Grave

Although the literature always refers to James Walbridge (1826–1913) as major, he was promoted to full colonel in 1863, which is why his headstone says colonel. He was born in Bennington near the Paper Mill covered bridge and was thirty-four when the war began. On May 3, 1861,

Grave of Major James Walbridge. *Author's collection.*

when Lincoln made his call for volunteers, Captain James H. Walbridge was appointed recruiting agent for the Second Vermont Regiment before taking command of Company A, formed by soldiers from Bennington. This was the first company of three-year men in the state. The regiment fought bravely at First Bull Run and later joined with the Third, Fourth, Fifth and Sixth Regiments to form the famous "Vermont Brigade." In one of the battles that led up to Antietam, Major Walbridge's troops were assigned to lead the attack on Crampton's Gap. One Vermont soldier reported to the *Bennington Banner*: "As we passed through Burkittsville we were cheered by the ladies of the town…We passed through the entire length of the village, the shot and shell of the enemy flying like Satan's angels over our heads." Although the Union forces broke through the Confederate lines at Crampton's Gap, General McClellan failed to follow up with an attack on the main body of Lee's army. Historians believe that had he done so, the terrible Battle of Antietam might never have taken place.

Major Walbridge distinguished himself at Fredericksburg, a battle in which he lost 107 men. So well respected was he that he was placed in command of the whole Vermont Brigade from February 1863 through April 1864, fighting in twenty-eight terrible battles, including Gettysburg. In 1864, a spinal difficulty forced him to resign his command, and he never fully recovered his health. Newton Stone then took over the brigade but was killed in the Battle of the Wilderness.

Few men have lived more exciting lives than James Walbridge. During his youth and early manhood, he fished for mackerel off the coast of Massachusetts and then became a California gold prospector, pioneer, printer and a member of the vigilance committee that took control of San Francisco in 1856 when it was still called the Barbary Coast. After the Civil War, he went to Panama, where he was superintendent of docks working for Trenor Park, who was then the president of the Panama Railroad Company. Major Walbridge died in North Bennington at the age of eighty-eight.

Notes

Slavery

1. Zirblis, *Friends*.
2. Vermont State Constitution, 1777.
3. Crockett, *Vermont*.
4. *Christian Register* 83, no. 48 (December 1, 1804).
5. Coffin, *Full Duty*, 28.
6. John Myers, "The Beginning of Antislavery Agencies in Vermont, 1832–1836," *Vermont History* (Summer 1968): 126–41.
7. Coffin, *Full Duty*, 31.
8. Zirblis, *Friends*.
9. Joseph Parks, "Uncovering the Underground Railroad," *Bennington Banner*, September 11–25, 1998.
10. Much of the information concerning the Hicks family is based on research conducted by Joe Hall, past president of the Bennington Historical Society.

Vermont Prepares for War

11. *Bennington Banner*, December 9, 1859; Coffin, *Full Duty*, 34.
12. Hiland Hall, Inaugural Address (in) *Journal of the House of Representatives*, October Session, 1858.

13. Crockett, *Vermont*, vol. 3, 495–504.
14. Population from the U.S. Census, various years.
15. Enlistment statistics from Waite, *Vermont*.
16. Coffin, *Full Duty*, 50.

War Is Declared

17. *Bennington Banner* April 18, 1861.
18. Ibid., April 24, 1861.
19. Coffin, *Full Duty*, 51.
20. Ibid., 24–25.

Bennington Volunteers for Duty

21. *Bennington Banner*, May 2, 1861.
22. Ibid., April 24, 1861.
23. Ibid., May 9, 1861.
24. Ibid., May 2, 1861.
25. Waite, *Vermont*, 61–62.
26. *Bennington Banner*, May 30, 1861.
27. Ibid., April 24, 1861.
28. Child, *Gazetteer*.
29. *Bennington Banner*, May 30, 1861.

Bennington Divided

30. Ibid., February 11, 1864.
31. http://www.firstepoch.com/articles/article05.asp; Dunaway, *Reminiscences*.

Recruiting and Filling the Ranks

32. The statistics for these and other regiments can be found in large part in Benedict, *Vermont*.

1861

33. *Bennington Banner*, June 13, 1861.
34. Ibid., June 20, 1861.
35. *Bennington Banner*, June 13, 1861.
36. Ibid., June 27, 1861.
37. Ibid., July 18, 1861.
38. Ibid., September 5, 1861.
39. Ibid., July 4, 1861.
40. Ibid., September 12, 1861.
41. Ibid., October 17, 1861.
42. Ibid., October 31, 1861.
43. Ibid., October 17, 1861.
44. Ibid., February 4, 1864.
45. Ibid., October 17, 1861.
46. *Troy Daily Times*, August 11, 1897.
47. *Bennington Banner*, October 31, 1861.
48. Ibid., October 17, 1861.

1862

49. Ibid., July 24, 1862.
50. Ibid.
51. http://www.johnflackwinslow.com.
52. *Bennington Banner*, August 14, 1862.
53. Ibid., July 24, 1862.
54. Ibid., August 14, 1862.
55. Ibid., August 28, 1862.
56. Ibid., September 25, 1862.
57. Ibid., October 9, 1862.
58. Ibid., October 30, 1862.
59. Ibid., October 23, 1862.
60. Ibid., December 11, 1862.
61. Ibid., October 23, 1862.
62. Ibid., February 19, 1863.

1863

63. Ibid., July 23, 1863.
64. Ibid., March 5, 1863.
65. Ibid., May 21, 1863.
66. Ibid., June 4, 1863.
67. Ibid., November 12, 1863.
68. Ibid., August 20, 1863.
69. Ibid., August 27, 1863.
70. Ibid., April 14, 1864.
71. Ibid., August 20, 1863.
72. Ibid., September 11, 1863.
73. Ibid.
74. Ibid., November 19, 1863.

1864

75. Ibid., May 1, 1862.
76. Ibid., January 7, 1864.
77. Ibid., March 24, 1864.
78. Ibid., February 4, 1864.
79. Ibid., January 14, 1864.
80. Ibid., May 12, 1864.
81. *Bennington Banner,* May 26, 1864.
82. Ibid., June 2, 1864.
83. Ibid., August 4, 1864.
84. Ibid., August 25, 1864.
85. Ibid., October 13, 1864.
86. Ibid., November 17, 1864.
87. Ibid., April 6, 1865.

1865

88. Ibid., December 15, 1864.
89. Ibid., April 13, 1865.
90. Ibid.
91. Ibid., April 27, 1865.

92. Ibid., June 29, 1865.
93. Ibid., August 17, 1865.

POSTSCRIPT

94. Information found in a letter from Varina Davis to Burton N. Harrison, November 1, 1867 in the Harrison Papers, Library of Congress.
95. *Bennington Banner,* October 1867.

OLD BENNINGTON

96. *Bennington Evening Banner,* February 19, 1906.
97. Many of these facts were taken from the Day Papers, a collection of clippings in the collection of the Bennington Museum Library.
98. Enlistment history for this and other soldiers was found in the http://VermontCivilWar.Org database devoted to Civil War veterans.
99. Coffin, *Full Duty*, 235–36.

BENNINGTON

100. *Bennington Banner,* June 16, 1982.
101. *History of the Soldiers' Home.*

NORTH BENNINGTON

102. Robinson, *Bennington*, 96.

Bibliography

Aldrich, Lewis Cass. *History of Bennington County, Vermont.* Syracuse, NY: D. Mason & Co., 1889.

Bacon, Mary Schell Hoke. *Old New England Churches and Their Children.* New York: Doubleday, Page & Co., 1906.

Beers, F.W. *Atlas of Bennington County Vermont.* New York: Beers, 1869.

Benedict, G.G. *Vermont in the Civil War.* 2 vols. Burlington, VT: Free Press Association, 1888.

Bennington Banner, 1861–1865.

Burleigh, Lucien. *Bennington, Vermont.* Troy, NY: Burleigh Lithograph Co., 1887.

Child, Hamilton, ed. *Gazetteer and Business Directory of Bennington County, VT.* Syracuse, NY: Journal Office, 1880.

Christian Register 83, no. 1 (January 7, 1804).

Coffin, Howard. *Full Duty: Vermonters in the Civil War.* Woodstock, VT: Countryman Press, 1993.

Conant, Edward. *Geography, History and Civil Government of Vermont.* Rutland, VT: Tuttle Co., 1890.

Crockett, Walter Hill. *Vermont: The Green Mountain State.* 3 vols. New York: Century History Co., 1921.

Davis, Varina to Burton N. Harrison. November 1, 1867. Harrison Papers. Library of Congress. Washington, D.C.

Day Papers. Bennington Museum Library. Bennington, VT.

The Dedication of the Bennington Battle Monument, and Celebration of the Hundredth Anniversary of the Admission of Vermont as a State. Bennington, VT: Banner Book and Job Printing House, 1892.

Dunaway, Wayland Fuller. *Reminiscences of a Rebel.* New York: Neale, 1913.

Hall, Hiland. "Inaugural Address." *Journal of the House of Representatives.* October session. 1858.

History of the Soldiers' Home of Vermont: 1884–2006. Bennington, VT: Soldiers' Home of Vermont, n.d.

Hubbard, Eleanor. "Vermont's Underground Railroad." *Vermont Historical Society Bulletin* 33, no. 2 (April 1965): 308–12.

Myers, John. "The Beginning of Antislavery Agencies in Vermont, 1832–1836." *Vermont History* (Summer 1968): 126–41.

Parks, Joseph. "Uncovering the Underground Railroad." *Bennington Banner,* September 11–25, 1998.

Presdee and Edwards. *Map of the Village of Bennington, Vermont.* New York: Presdee & Edwards, 1852.

Rice, E., and C.E. Harwood. *Map of Bennington Country, Vermont.* New York: C.B. Peckham, 1856.

Robinson, Melvin H., ed. *Bennington Souvenir 1904.* Bennington, VT: YMCA, 1904.

Spargo, John. *The Potters and Potteries of Bennington.* Bennington, VT: Bennington Museum, 1926.

Ullery, Jacob G. *Men of Vermont.* Brattleboro, VT: Transcript Pub. Co., 1894.

United States Census, various years.

Vermont in the Civil War. http://vermontcivilwar.org.

Vermont State Constitution, 1777.

Waite, Otis F.R. *Vermont in the Great Rebellion.* Claremont, NH: Tracy, Chase & Co., 1869.

Zirblis, Raymond Paul. *Friends of Freedom: The Vermont Underground Railroad Survey Report.* Montpelier: Vermont Department of State Buildings and Vermont Division for Historic Preservation, 1996.

Index

U

V

W

Y

About the Author

Bill Morgan is a writer, librarian and archival consultant who lives in Bennington, Vermont. In addition to being the president of the Bennington Historical Society, he is also the author of dozens of books and travel guides. Currently, he is working on the *Civil War Lover's Guide to New York City*, which will be published later this year. His most recent books include *The Typewriter Is Holy: The Complete, Uncensored History of the Beat Generation* (Simon & Schuster, 2010) and *I Celebrate Myself: The Somewhat Private Life of Allen Ginsberg* (Viking, 2006).

Photo by Chris Felver.

Visit us at
www.historypress.net

This title is also available as an e-book